First World War
and Army of Occupation
War Diary
France, Belgium and Germany

63 (ROYAL NAVAL) DIVISION
188 Infantry Brigade
Royal Irish Regiment
2nd Battalion
1 May 1918 - 2 May 1919

WO95/3111/3

The Naval & Military Press Ltd
www.nmarchive.com
Published in association with The National Archives

Published by

The Naval & Military Press Ltd

Unit 10 Ridgewood Industrial Park,

Uckfield, East Sussex,

TN22 5QE England

Tel: +44 (0) 1825 749494

www.naval-military-press.com

www.nmarchive.com

This diary has been reprinted in facsimile from the original. Any imperfections are inevitably reproduced and the quality may fall short of modern type and cartographic standards.

© Crown Copyright
Images reproduced by permission of The National Archives, London, England, 2015.

Contents

Document type	Place/Title	Date From	Date To
Heading	WO95/3111-3		
Heading	63rd Division 188th Infy Bde 2nd Bn Roy Irish Regt 1918-May 1919 From 16 Div 49 Bde		
War Diary	Raincheval	01/05/1918	01/05/1918
War Diary	Forceville	07/05/1918	07/05/1918
War Diary	Englebelmer	13/05/1918	26/05/1918
War Diary	Forceville	30/05/1918	31/05/1918
Operation(al) Order(s)	2nd Bn. The Royal Irish Regt Order No.2		
Operation(al) Order(s)	2nd Bn The Royal Irish Regt Order No.3	12/05/1918	12/05/1918
Miscellaneous	Preliminary Report On Raid Carried Out By Anson Bn. On Night May 24th/25th	25/05/1919	25/05/1919
War Diary	Forceville	01/06/1918	05/06/1918
War Diary	Herissart	05/06/1918	23/06/1918
War Diary	Acheux	23/06/1918	30/06/1918
War Diary	Herissart	05/06/1918	05/06/1918
Operation(al) Order(s)	2nd Bn The Royal Irish Regt Order No.8	04/06/1918	04/06/1918
Miscellaneous	2nd Bn The Royal Irish Regt Order No.10	22/06/1918	22/06/1918
Miscellaneous	2nd Bn The Royal Irish Regt Order No.4	19/05/1918	19/05/1918
Heading	2 R Irish Regt Vol 40 July 1918		
Miscellaneous	Report On Raid Night 19/20 July Carried Out By 2nd Royal Irish Regt		
Map	Map		
Heading	Cover For Documents. Nature Of Enclosures. Report on Raid on Crater in Q.10.b and Adjoining Trenches by 2nd Royal Irish Regiment Night 19th/20th July 1918		
War Diary	Acheux	01/07/1918	01/07/1918
War Diary	P.15.b & D.	06/07/1918	06/07/1918
War Diary	P.16.a.c	06/07/1918	25/07/1918
War Diary	Raincheval	25/07/1918	28/07/1918
War Diary	St Leger	29/07/1918	29/07/1918
Miscellaneous	63rd (R.N.) Division No.GA.5/30	24/07/1918	24/07/1918
Miscellaneous	B.M.1751	22/07/1918	22/07/1918
Miscellaneous	188th Infantry Brigade Report On Raid On Crater In Q.10.b. And Adjoining Trenches By 2nd Royal Irish Regt Night Of July 19th/20th 1918	21/07/1918	21/07/1918
Miscellaneous	Section II Plan	22/07/1918	22/07/1918
Miscellaneous	Section III Execution	21/07/1918	21/07/1918
Map	Tracing To Accompany Left		
Miscellaneous	Report On Machine Gun Action In Raid On Night Of 19th/29th July	21/07/1918	21/07/1918
Miscellaneous	Section IV Notes And Lessons	21/07/1918	21/07/1918
Operation(al) Order(s)	188th Inf. Brigade Order No.204	17/07/1918	17/07/1918
Miscellaneous	Appendix IV to 188th Infantry Brigade Order No.204 Administrative Arrangements		
Operation(al) Order(s)	2nd Battalion The Royal Irish Regiment Order No.17		
Map	Map		
Miscellaneous	2nd Battalion The Royal Irish Regt		
Miscellaneous	Special Order Issued To "D" Company To Supplement Battalion Order No.17 Which Has Been Read Out And Fully Explained To All Ranks	19/07/1918	19/07/1918

Type	Description	Date 1	Date 2
Operation(al) Order(s)	63rd (RN) Division Order No.249	15/07/1918	15/07/1918
Miscellaneous	63rd (RN) Division No.GA.5/30/5	19/07/1918	19/07/1918
Operation(al) Order(s)	63rd (R.N.) Divisional Artillery Operation Order No.208	16/07/1918	16/07/1918
Miscellaneous	63rd (R.N.) Div. Arty. Tasks (To Accompany 63rd D.A.Operation Order No.208		
Miscellaneous	42nd Div. Arty. Tasks (To Accompany 63rd D.A. Operation Order No.208)		
Miscellaneous	38th (Welsh) Div. Arty. Tasks (To Accompany 63rd D.A. Operation Order No.208)		
Miscellaneous	Heavy Artillery Tasks (To Accompany 63rd Div. Arty. Operation Order No.208)		
Operation(al) Order(s)	188th L.T.M. Battery-Order No.14	18/07/1918	18/07/1918
Miscellaneous	Left Artillery Group 63rd (RN) Division	18/07/1918	18/07/1918
Operation(al) Order(s)	63rd (RN) Machine Gun Battalion Operation Order No.44	16/07/1918	16/07/1918
Diagram etc	Diagram		
Map	Map I		
Map	Map 2		
Map	Map		
Map	France		
Miscellaneous	Appendix No.1		
Miscellaneous	Appendix No.2		
Operation(al) Order(s)	2nd Bn The Royal Irish Regt Order No.31	12/07/1918	12/07/1918
Operation(al) Order(s)	2/Rd Regt Operation Order No.30	16/07/1918	16/07/1918
Miscellaneous	O.O No.10	18/07/1918	18/07/1918
Miscellaneous	63rd (RN) Division	09/07/1918	09/07/1918
Miscellaneous	All Batteries & Detd. Sections (317th.Bde) etc.	10/07/1918	10/07/1918
Miscellaneous	Report For Raid On Crater In Q.10.b		
Miscellaneous	63rd Division No.G.A5/30	26/07/1918	26/07/1918
Miscellaneous	Third Army No.G. 12/293	28/07/1918	28/07/1918
Miscellaneous	Detailed Plan For Raid On Crater In C.10.b. And Adjoining Trenches	15/07/1918	15/07/1918
Map	Tracing "A"		
Diagram etc	Tracing "B"		
Map	Tracing "C"		
Miscellaneous	63rd (RN) Division	22/07/1918	22/07/1918
Miscellaneous	188th Infantry Brigade Report On Raid On Crater In Q.10.b And Adjoining Trenches By 2nd Royal Irish Regt Night Of July 19th/20th 1918	21/07/1918	21/07/1918
Miscellaneous	Report On Raid On Crater In Q.10.b And Adjoining Trenches By 2nd Royal Irish Regiment-Night 19/20th July 1918		
Miscellaneous	Section II Plan	22/07/1918	22/07/1918
Miscellaneous	Appendices B.D and G Forwards to 63 (RN) Division only		
Operation(al) Order(s)	188th Inf. Brigade Order No.204	17/07/1918	17/07/1918
Miscellaneous	Appendix IV to 188th Infantry Brigade Order No.204		
Map	Map		
Operation(al) Order(s)	2nd Battalion The Royal Irish Regiment Order No.17	18/07/1918	18/07/1918
Miscellaneous	Amendment No.1 To 2nd Royal Irish Regiment Order No. 17	18/07/1918	18/07/1918
Miscellaneous	Lt Sanderson		
Diagram etc	Moonlight Chart For July August @ September 1918		
Miscellaneous	2nd Battalion The Royal Irish Regt		

Type	Description	Date 1	Date 2
Miscellaneous	Special Order Issued To "D" Company To Supplement Battalion Order No.17 Which Has Been Read Out And Fully Explained To All Ranks	19/07/1918	19/07/1918
Miscellaneous	B.M 1795	25/07/1918	25/07/1918
Operation(al) Order(s)	63rd (R.N.) Divisional Artillery Operation Order No.208	16/07/1918	16/07/1918
Miscellaneous	63rd (R.N.) Div. Arty. Tasks (To Accompany 63rd D.A.Operation Order No.208)		
Miscellaneous	42nd Div. Arty. Tasks (To Accompany 63rd D.A.Operation Order No.208)		
Miscellaneous	38th (Welsh) Div. Arty. Tasks (To Accompany 63rd D.A. Operation Order No.208)		
Miscellaneous	Heavy Artillery Tasks (To Accompany 63rd Div. Arty. Operation Order No.208)		
Miscellaneous	Amendment No.3 To Operation Order No. 44	18/07/1918	18/07/1918
Miscellaneous	Amendment No.1 To 63rd (RN) M.G. Battn. Operation Order No.44	16/07/1918	16/07/1918
Operation(al) Order(s)	63rd (RN) Machine Gun Battalion Operation Order No.44	16/07/1918	16/07/1918
Map	63rd (RN) M.G. Bn. Map With O.O. 44		
Operation(al) Order(s)	188th L.T.M. Battery Order No.14	18/07/1918	18/07/1918
Miscellaneous	Left Artillery Group (63rd (R.N.) Division)	18/07/1918	18/07/1918
Miscellaneous	Report On Artillery Operations Connected With The Raid On Night 19th/20th July	21/07/1918	21/07/1918
Map	Trace To Accompany Left Group Arty Order		
Miscellaneous	Report On Machine Gun Action In Raid On Night Of 19th/29th July	21/07/1918	21/07/1918
Miscellaneous	Section III-Execution Report On Special Operations In Connection With Raid By 2nd Royal Irish Regiment On Night 19th/20th July	20/07/1918	20/07/1918
Miscellaneous	Section III Execution	21/07/1918	21/07/1918
Miscellaneous	Section IV Notes And Lessons	21/07/1918	21/07/1918
Miscellaneous	C Form Messages And Signals		
Miscellaneous	2/R. Ir. Regt.	31/07/1918	31/07/1918
Miscellaneous	V Corps No.GS.456/11	20/07/1918	20/07/1918
Map	Map		
Miscellaneous	Appendix No 8		
Miscellaneous	2nd Rl. Irish Regt. Defence Scheme (Provisional)		
Heading	2 R Irish Rgt. Vol 41 April 1918		
War Diary	St Leger	01/08/1918	04/08/1918
War Diary	Louvencourt	05/08/1918	08/08/1918
War Diary	Contay	08/08/1918	15/08/1918
War Diary	Henu	16/08/1918	28/08/1918
War Diary	Miraumont RW	30/08/1918	30/08/1918
Operation(al) Order(s)	Battalion Routine Orders No. 757	03/08/1918	03/08/1918
Miscellaneous	188th Inf. Brigade Warning Order No. 222	31/08/1918	31/08/1918
Miscellaneous			
War Diary	Boileux-Au-Mont	01/09/1918	01/09/1918
War Diary	Fontaine 9.No	02/09/1918	02/09/1918
War Diary	Hendecourt	02/09/1918	02/09/1918
War Diary	Bois-De-Bouche	03/09/1918	07/09/1918
War Diary	Croisilles	08/09/1918	08/09/1918
War Diary	Gouy-En-Artois	09/09/1918	09/09/1918
War Diary	Croiselles	26/09/1918	26/09/1918
War Diary	Queant	27/09/1918	27/09/1918
War Diary	Graincourt	28/09/1918	28/09/1918

War Diary	Cantaing	29/09/1918	29/09/1918
War Diary	High Sconnal S of Cambrai	30/09/1918	30/09/1918
Miscellaneous	2nd Bn The Royal Irish Regt	17/09/1918	17/09/1918
Operation(al) Order(s)	2nd Royal Irish Regiment Order No.32	16/09/1918	16/09/1918
War Diary		01/10/1918	13/10/1918
War Diary	Croisette	13/10/1918	30/10/1918
War Diary	32 B 13 Sheets	01/11/1918	11/11/1918
War Diary	Sriennes	12/11/1918	27/11/1918
War Diary	Blaregnies	28/11/1918	30/11/1918
Miscellaneous	2nd Royal Irish Regiment Summary Of Events From 9/11/18 To 11/11/18	12/11/1918	12/11/1918
Miscellaneous	63rd Div. Arty.		
Miscellaneous	Special Order Of The Day By Lieut Colonel M.C.C. Harrison D.S.O. M Commanding 2nd Bn. The Royal Irish Regiment	13/11/1918	13/11/1918
Miscellaneous	To All Ranks Of The 188th Infantry Brigade	12/11/1918	12/11/1918
Operation(al) Order(s)	2nd Bn The Royal Irish Regiment Order No.33	26/11/1918	26/11/1918
Miscellaneous	To All Ranks Of 188th Infantry Brigade	27/11/1918	27/11/1918
War Diary	Blaregnies	01/12/1918	08/12/1918
War Diary	Frameries	14/12/1918	02/05/1919

WD05/3111 (3)

63RD DIVISION
188TH INFY BDE

2ND BN ROY. IRISH REGT
MAY 1918 – MAY 1919

FRom 16 div
49 BdE

WAR DIARY or INTELLIGENCE SUMMARY. 2nd R.M. REGT.

Vol 38

Place	Date	Hour	Summary of Events and Information	Remarks and references to Appendices
RAINCHEVAL	918		Battalion at rest: H.Q., "A", "B" & "D" Coys under Canvas at RAINCHEVAL. "C" Coy in Billets at ARQUEVES.	
	7th		During this period two Platoons Nos 3 & 16 took part in a musketry Competition run in the Brigade: another feature of the training carried out was a demonstration by a Platoon of "B" Coy under LT SMITH of a Platoon in the attack. Working parties 300 strong were supplied daily to work on the FOREEVILLE defences.	
FOREEVILLE	7th		The 63rd (R.N.) Division relieve the 17th Division in the Centre Sector of the V Corps front. The Battalion relieving the 10th Lancashire Fusiliers Batt: H.Q. "A", "C" & "D" Coys at FOREEVILLE. "B" Coy in PURPLE LINE in front of ENGLEBELMER.	See Appendix No 1
ENGLEBELMER	13th		Battalion relieves the 1st Royal Marine Battalion in support and moves to ENGLEBELMER	" No 2
	19-20		Battalion relieves the 1st Royal Marine Battalion in the front line of the HAMEL Sector without support. "A" Coy Right, "C" Coy Left, "B" Coy Reserve and base line. Disposition	" No 3
ENGLEBELMER	23		Battalion is relieved by the ANSON Batt: and proceeds to ENGLEBELMER	26 G
	24		A Raid which proved successful is carried out by the ANSON Batt. 2 Coys of the 2nd Portugal Inch Regt. are placed at the disposal of the C.O. R. ANSON Batt.	(2ahaln)

WAR DIARY
or
INTELLIGENCE SUMMARY.
(Erase heading not required.)

Army Form C. 2118.

Place	Date	Hour	Summary of Events and Information	Remarks and references to Appendices
ENGLEBELMER	1918 May 24		to hold the front line during the Raid. 1 Platoon was also detailed to act as Stretcher Bearers and another to take charge of Prisoners. {A patrol of D Coy under 2nd Lieut M.M. Brown ascertained the enemy's strength & dispositions, information regarding which proved to be accurate in	
	26		Very heavy shelling of Battalion H.Q. and vicinity during the period. On the 26th very great detail just a direct hit on the advanced Orderly Room caused great damage.	but in fortune "A" R.A.M.C
FOREEVILLE	30		Battalion is relieved by the Anson Battn. and proceeds to FOREEVILLE in reserve. Coy. being left in PURPLE LINE at ENGLEBELMER. On the whole the work during the month was exceptionally fine with the exception of the night of the 19th-20th May which was one it is without a record.	

HONOURS and AWARDS.

Lt Col. N.C.C. HARRISON — Silver Medal for Military Valour (Italy)
         do   do   — M.C.
CAPT. B.J. CLANCY   — M.C.
2/Lt D.T. McWEENEY (On Rev.) — M.C.
No 7805 Pte PHELAN, C "B" Coy — M.M.
" 10652   " O'BRIEN, P "D" Coy — M.M.

Army Form C. 2118.

WAR DIARY
or
INTELLIGENCE SUMMARY.
(Erase heading not required.)

Place	Date	Hour	Summary of Events and Information	Remarks and references to Appendices
	1918. May		HONOURS and AWARDS (cont'd)	
	1		No 693 Pte GREGORY, W. — M.M.	
			CASUALTIES and DEPARTURES. OFFICERS	
	14		2/Lt W.H. BROWNE (Con Pam.) to 188th Bde L.T.M.B.	
	20		" H.T. McCULLAGH Wounded in Action.	
	23		" D.T. McWEENEY to Hospital.	
	"		" F.W. BANKS to Hospital.	
			CASUALTIES and DEPARTURES. OTHER RANKS.	
	1		39 O.R. to Base for Re-classification	
	13		1 " Wounded in Action	
	14		2 " Do	
	15		2 " Do	
	16		2 " Do	
	17		2 " Do	
	19		1 " Killed in Action.	

WAR DIARY
or
INTELLIGENCE SUMMARY.

Army Form C. 2118.

Place	Date	Hour	Summary of Events and Information	Remarks and references to Appendices
	1918 May		CASUALTIES & DEPARTURES O.R. (cont?)	
	19		6 O.R. Wounded in Action	
	20		2 " Killed in Action	
			3 " Wounded in Action	
	22		2 " " do	
	23		2 " " do	
	25		6 " " do	
	26		1 " " do	
	27		3 " " do	
	28		1 " Killed in Action	
			1 " Wounded in Action	
	31		2 " " do	

Army Form C. 2118.

WAR DIARY
or
INTELLIGENCE SUMMARY.

(Erase heading not required.)

Instructions regarding War Diaries and Intelligence Summaries are contained in F. S. Regs., Part II. and the Staff Manual respectively. Title pages will be prepared in manuscript.

Place	Date	Hour	Summary of Events and Information	Remarks and references to Appendices
	1918 May		REINFORCEMENTS OFFICERS	
	3		2/Lt N.M. CHEVERS	
	"		" J.E. LOWRY	
	"		" J.D. KELLY	
	"		" H.T. McCULLAGH	
	"		" M.J. MEANEY	
	"		" F.W. BANKS	
	"		Lt R.E.W. BURKE. M.C.	
	8		" T. HUGHES (Con. Rangers)	
	23		" J.H.A. NEVILL (Spec. List)	
	25		2/Lt J. COADY (Con. Rangers) at Div" WING.	
	31			
			OTHER RANKS	
	9		52 O.R. from 4th Batt. R.Dub. Irish Regt	
	21		32 " " " " "	
	23		10 " " " " "	
	28		0	
	29		0	

M.C.C. Harrison Lieut. Colonel
Commanding 2nd Batt. Royal Irish Regt.
2/6/18.

Appendix No 1

SECRET   COPY No.

2ND. BN. THE ROYAL IRISH REGT. ORDER No 2.

Ref: 1/40,000 - 57 D.

1. The 63rd Division will relieve the 17th Division in the centre sector of the V Corps front tomorrow, the 7th inst.

2. The Battn. will relieve the 10th Hyde Hrs. in reserve. H.Qrs. F.22.a.6.2. 3 coys in front of FORCEVILLE, 1 coy in SUPPORT line in front of ENGLEBELMER.

3. "A" Coy of this Regt. will relieve "D" Coy 10th Camn. Fus.
   "B" "   "   "   "   "   "   "A" "   "   "   "
   "C" "   "   "   "   "   "   "C" "   "   "   "
   "D" "   "   "   "   "   "   "B" "   "   "   "

4. The Battn. (less "B" and "C" Coys) will parade at 8.30am tomorrow, and will march by Coys at 2 minutes interval via RAINCHEVAL & RAINEDES to FORCEVILLE. Order of march "A", "D", "C" Nbn. "C" Coy will pass Starting Point, ACHEUX mill at 9.35 am - 150 yds after "D" Coy. "B" Coy will remain in camp and will march off under orders to be issued by O.C. "B" Coy - they will not reach F.22.d.9.2. till 12.30 p.m.

5. Transport arrangements: 1 L.G. limber per coy - 1 L.G. limber for H.Qrs. - mules and mess carts and 1 limber for Officers' kits will be on football ground by 8am. Officers' valises, trench kits etc, will be stacked separately by the Guard room by 8am.

6. All trench stores, trench maps, aeroplane photographs, defence and work schemes will be taken over carefully.

7. Attention is called to 63rd Div. Trench Standing Orders.

8. Relief complete will be reported by Coys - using Coy. Runners meanwhile.

9. Every man with the exception of Signallers, runners and Nos 1 and 2 of L. Guns, will be equipped with 170 rounds S.A.A.

10. Instructions regarding transport will be issued separately.

11. Each Coy. will bring 5 Lewis Guns with them and the SAA's of same.

The Lewis Gun Officer will arrange the necessary teams to man the 4 Lewis Guns at Bn.Hdrs. – these men will parade with Bn.Hdrs. at 8.30 am.

12. Guides for Bn. Hdrs, "A", "C" and "D" Coys. will be at CrossRoads - R.21.d.3.7.

13. The cookers for "A", "C" and "D" Coys. will accompany their Coys.

14. ACKNOWLEDGE

Roberts
Capt. & Adjt.
2/ The Rl. Irish Regiment.

Issued at 6 pm
Copy No.1. HQ 188th Bde.   Copy No.7. L.G. Officer
    2. Second in Command   8. Sig. Officer
    3. O/C "A" Coy   9. Medical Officer
    4. " "B" "   10. Q.M.
    5. " "C" "   11. Transport Officer
    6. " "D" "   12. R.S.M.
       Copy No. 13. File.

__Addendum__. "C" Coys Lewis Gun limber will be at "C" Coy HQ by 8.30 am.

In addition, the Transport Officer will detail one limber to report "C" Coys HQ by 6.30 am to convey "C" Coy Officers Kits etc to camp.

J.G.

SECRET   Appendix No. 2.
          COPY NO ____
2nd Bn THE ROYAL IRISH REGT. ORDER No 3. 12-5-18
REF. TRENCH. MAP.

1. The Battn will relieve the 1/R.M. Battn in support tomorrow the 13th inst.

2. "D" Coy 2/R.I. Regt will relieve "C" Coy 1/R.M. Battn
   "B" "   "   "   "   "   "B"   "   "   "
   "A" "   "   "   "   "   "A"   "   "   "
   "C" "   "   "   "   "   "D"   "   "   "

3. Advance parties consisting of 1 OFFICER per Coy, 1 NCO per Coy, Bn GAS NCO, 2 H.Q. RUNNERS, 1 NCO per platoon and NCS 1 of L.Gs teams will parade at Bn HQrs at 9AM in fighting order, and will take over positions, trench stores etc during daylight; Map references of Coy H QRs 1/R.M. Battn will be given to all concerned.

4. GUIDES, 1 per platoon from 1/R.M. Battn will be at GREEN BUSH P.29. a.35.65. (on the road due W of the Small rectangular wood) at 8 p.m.

5. Coys will move off from present positions by platoons at 3 minutes interval.
   Order of march :— "C". "A". "B". Bn HQrs.
   Leading platoon of "C" Coy will move off at 7.30 p.m.

6. "D" COY (in WHITE LINE) will make all arrangements for relief direct with O/C 1/R.M. Battn

7. TRANSPORT. Maltese Cart, Mess Cart, 2 limbers for cooking utensils, 1 limber for Bn. H.Q. will be at Bn HQrs at 7 P.M. Horses for Cookers will be there at the same time. 1 limber will be placed at the disposal of the O/C "D" Coy. This limber will be at "D" Coys. H.Qrs by 8 P.M.

8. RATIONS will not reach ration dumps before 10.30 P.M.

8/ All parties will be checked by Coys, CLEARLY LABELLED on the bottom, with owners REGT. NO, NAME, and COY, at Bn H.Q'S by 3 P.M. The T.O. will arrange the necessary Transport.

9/ Guides for ANSON BATTN will be supplied if required by the O/C. ANSON BATTN.

10/ Trench Stores, Trench maps, Tools, Aeroplane photographs, will be carefully taken over and receipts obtained. Receipts to Orderly Room by 9 a.m the 14th inst.

11/ Completion of relief will be notified to Bn H.Q. by the code message "NOT UNDERSTOOD"

12/ The AID POST will be established at :—

___

ACKNOWLEDGE.

Captain & Adjutant
2/ The Royal Irish Regt.

Issued at ——
Copy No 1. A.Q. 118 BDE.
     2 O/c 1. R.M. Bn
     3 O/c ANSON Bn
     4 Second in Command.
     5 O/c "A" COY
     6 . "B" .
     7

Copy No 8 O/c "C" COY
     9 . "D" .
     10 L.G. OFFICER
     11 SIGS. OFFICER
     12 MED. OFFICER
     13 Q.M.S
     14 T. POST OFFICER

Copy No 15. R.S.M.
     16 FILE.

10/. All trench stores, reserve water, etc., will be carefully handed and taken over. and Trench Store Lists rendered to Bn. H.Q. by 9 am. 20th inst.

11/. Completion of relief will be reported to Bn H.Q. using code word message "REQUIRE WATER."

                Capt., & Adjt.,
      2/ Royal Irish Regt.

Issued at ———

Copy No. 1	H.Q. 188 Bde	Copy No. 9	L.G. Offr.
2	O/C 1/RM Bn	10	Sig. Offr.
3	" ANSON Bn.	11	Med. Offr.
4	Sec-in-Command	12	Q.M.
5	O/C "A" Coy	13	T.O.
6	" "B" "	14	R.S.M.
7	" "C" "	15	War Diary
8	" "D" "	16	File.

B.M. 1093.

S E C R E T.

Preliminary Report on Raid carried out by Anson Bn. on night May 24th/25th.

This report is partly based on the report of men seen in the line this morning, who took part in the raid, and may be inaccurate in some of the details. A full report will be forwarded as soon as reports can be obtained from the Officers who took part in the operations.

The men were able, in most cases, to line up for the raid before Zero, outside our Front Line Trench, on account of the mist and consequent darkness of the night.

The advance towards the initial barrage was made punctually at 11-15 p.m., there being no delay, as most of the men were already out of the trench.

The enemy barrage came down at Zero plus 4 minutes on our Front Line. Some shells came over at Zero plus 1 minute but these were probably an enemy crash fired at 11-15 p.m.

All ranks state that the artillery and Stokes Mortar barrage was very accurate and, on the left, so terrified the enemy that some of them ran straight to our lines to give themselves up.

The enemy were numerous but were in great confusion and many were seen running into our barrage.

The chief resistance met was from enemy Machine Guns, each manned by a crew of 5 men, but these were quickly overpowered by our men following close behind the barrage. The enemy's casualties are believed to have been heavy.

Men of the right and centre Companies state that they reached the railway. Of these two Companies the right appears to have met with the greatest opposition. It is understood that the HOOD Battn. on our right encountered great opposition in traversing the ground raided by the R.M. Battalion on the night May 18th/19th, which, although on the previous occasion was unoccupied, was held in strength last night.

The left Company seems to have been uniformly successful. After overpowering the enemy in the Orchard, an advance was made to the second objectives which were quickly reached, prisoners being taken and many of the enemy killed.

One platoon pushed forward, according to plan, and occupied the bank above the suspected H.Q. at Q.23.b.9.6. Reports from the Special Platoon and the Platoon of 'A' Company told off for the capture of these H.Q. have not yet been received. It is understood that these patrols met strong forces of the enemy who offered much resistance. The raiders returned to our trenches by 1-45 a.m.

Our casualties were approximately 70 all ranks, of which 1 Officer and 9 O.R. were killed and 5 Officers wounded.

1 Officer and 22 O.R. of the 87th. R.I.R. were captured together with 7 Machine Guns (probably 8).

The enemy's call for Artillery support was a double red light, and floating white lights, believed to be attached to small anchored balloons, were seen as on the occasion of the previous raid just east of the ANCRE.

The chief damage done to our trenches was at Q.22.b.9.5., Q.23.a.4.5., Q.23.c.1.8. Q.23.c.5.1.

The enemy has shown more than his usual activity on our Front System this morning, especially on Communication Trenches, with 5.9" and 4.2" H.E. shells.

T.D. Coleridge.

Brigadier General,
Commanding -
189th. Inf. Brigade.

25/5/18.

WAR DIARY
of
INTELLIGENCE SUMMARY.

(Erase heading not required.)

Army Form C. 2118.

2/R Irish Regt

Place	Date	Hour	Summary of Events and Information	Remarks and references to Appendices
	1918			
FORCEVILLE	June 1st	5ᵖᵐ	Battalion in Brigade Reserve at FORCEVILLE. The 63ʳᵈ (R.N.) Division is relieved by the 38ᵗʰ (Welsh) Division the Battalion being relieved by the 16ᵗʰ Royal Welsh Fusiliers and moving into Billets at HERISSART.	See Appendix No. 1.
HERISSART	5–23		Battalion at HERISSART undergoing Training. During this period 6 successful Battalion Sports were held, also Grand throwing Competitions which were entered into with the greatest enthusiasm. Brigade Sports were also held. Inspection of Transport by the Corps and Divisional Commanders. During the period Anti-Aircraft Lewis Gun Guards were found over Corps Ammunition dump.	
	23.		The 63ʳᵈ (R.N.) Division relieves the 17ᵗʰ Division in the Left (MAILLY) Sector of the V Corps, the Battalion relieving the 10ᵗʰ Sherwood Foresters in the BROWN LINE at ACHEUX.	See Appendix No. 2.
ACHEUX	23–30		Battalion in Brigade Reserve.	

WAR DIARY
or
INTELLIGENCE SUMMARY.
(Erase heading not required.)

Army Form C. 2118.

Place	Date	Hour	Summary of Events and Information	Remarks and references to Appendices
HERISSART	1918. June 5		HONOURS and AWARDS.	
			Lt. Col. M.C.C. HARRISON .... M.C.	
			CAPT. W.C.V. GALWEY, M.C. ..... Bar to M.C.	
			" B.J. CLANCY .... M.C.	
			2/Lt. R.T. HAMILTON .... M.C.	
			N° 698 Pte GREGORY, W. .... M.M.	
			" 8610 Sergt BOYLE, J. .... M.M.	
			" 10573 Pte FLEMING, G. .... M.M.	
			" 11551 Sergt NIXON, J. .... M.M.	
			" 10652 Pte O'BRIEN, P. .... M.M.	
			" 11034 L/Cpl O'CONNORS, M. .... M.M.	
			" 3584 Pte McEVOY, P. .... M.M.	
			" 18236 " WILLIAMS, A. .... M.M.	

Army Form C. 2118.

WAR DIARY
or
INTELLIGENCE SUMMARY.
(Erase heading not required.)

Place	Date	Hour	Summary of Events and Information	Remarks and references to Appendices
HERISSART	6/18		REINFORCEMENTS OFFICERS.	
			CAPT. A.V. BRIDGE 5-6-18	
			2/Lt W.C.D. GIFFIN 5-6-18	
			CAPT. O'NEIL SEGRAVE 14-6-18	
			O. RANKS Nil	
			M.C. Harrison Lt. Col.	
			Comdt. 2nd R. Irish Regt	

Appendix No. 1

Secret.   Copy No. ......

2nd Bn. The Royal Irish Regt. Order No. 8.

Reference Map:- Sheet 57 D. 1/40.000.   The Field, 4-6-1918.

1. The 63rd. (R.N) Div. is being relieved by the 38th. (Welsh) Div. The relief will be completed by the morning of June 6th. 1918.

2. The 188th Inf. Bde. will be relieved in the MESNIL LEFT SECTOR by the 113th Inf. Bde. on June 5th & 6th. 1918, and will move to HERISSART less R.M. Bn.

3. The Bn. will be relieved by the 16th R.W.F. tomorrow, June 5th. Relief of 3 coys and H.Q. at FORCEVILLE to be complete by 4 p.m. Relief of "C" Coy not to commence before 9.30 p.m.

4. "A", "B", "D" Coys, & Bn. H.Q. will march off independently immediately they are relieved.- Route:- "A" Track running South of FORCEVILLE. VARENNES - HARPONVILLE - TOUTENCOURT.

5. All movements:- (a) East of the line ACHEUX - VARENNES will be by platoons at 200 yds. distance.

(b) Between the line ACHEUX - VARENNES and TOUTENCOURT - by Coys. at 200 yds. distance.

Similar distances to be maintained between corresponding units of transport.

6. On being relieved by a Coy. 16th R.W.F., "C" Coy will move to billets in HERISSART under arrangements to be made by O.C. "C" Coy.

7. The 113th Inf. Bde. are sending forward advance parties of 1 Officer and 1 N.C.O. per Coy for troops in and forward of the PURPLE SYSTEM, on the morning of June 5th.

8. 4 Guides from "C" Coy will be at Bn. H.Q. at 8.30 p.m on the 5th inst.

9. Billeting Party: consisting of Lt. W.H. SANDERSON and 5 B.O.R. 1/Sgts. will meet Staff Capt. at 12 noon on 5th inst at the Town Major's Office, HERISSART. They will carry 24 hrs rations as they will pass the night at HERISSART. They will meet their coys on "A" track as it comes into Northern end of HERISSART.

10. Transport. L.G. limbers for Bn. HQ, "A", "B" and "D" Coys, mess cart, mother cart, 1 limber, horses for cookers, will be at Bn. HQ. at 2 p.m. on 5th inst. 2 limbers to be at "C" Coys HQ. at 9.30 p.m.

2

11. Relief complete will be reported as follows :-
(a) By "A", "B" & "D" Coys. - to Bn. HQ. by runner
(b) By O.C. "C" Coy. to Bde. HQ. using code word phrase "NO PETROL TINS."

12. Officers valises, etc, will be stacked at Orderly Room by 2 pm. T.O. to arrange transport.

13. All trenches, billets, bivouacs, tents must be left scrupulously clean. Certificates that they are so will be obtained from incoming units and forwarded to Bn. HQ. by 3 pm, on the 6th inst.

14. Trench stores will be carefully handed over - particularly ammunitions, etc in the PURPLE LINE.

15. 4 Coys 2/R.I. Regt., please ACKNOWLEDGE

            [signature]
            Capt. & Adjt.
            2nd Bn. The Royal Irish Regiment

Issued at 6 pm.

Copies to :-
No. 1. 188th Bde. HQ.   No. 9. Med. Offr.
    2. O.C, 16 R.W.F.   10. A.M.
    3. 2nd in Command   11. T. O.
    4. OC "A" Coy   12. L. Sgt Masson
    5. " "B" "   13. R. S. M.
    6. " "C" "   14. War Diary
    7. " "D" "   15. File
    8. Sig. Offr.   16. Spare

Appendix N.2.

Secret.   Copy no.
      2nd. Bn. The Royal Irish Regt. Order no. 10.
Reference 1/40.000 - 57. D.
                                    The Field. 22nd. June 1916.

1. The 63rd. (RN) Division was transferred from the XXII Corps to the V Corps from noon June 19th., and is now in G.H.Q. Reserve at 9 hours notice to move.

2. The 63rd. (RN) Division (less Artillery) will relieve the 17th. Division (less Artillery) in the left (MAILLY) Sector of the V Corps Front, the relief to be complete by 6.00 a.m. on 22st the same on June 23rd.

3. The 188th. Inf. Bde. will relieve the 51st Inf. Bde. in Reserve.

4. The Bde. will relieve the 10th. SHERWOOD FORESTERS in the BROWN LINE area — P. 15. B. and D. and P. 16. a. and c.

5. Advance parties consisting of 1 Officer per coy., Bndt. Offr., 1 H.Q. per Coy., 1 n.c.o. per platoon, 1 intelligent guide per Coy., Bn. Sgn. N.C.O., will parade at the Cashelry Room at 9 a.m. and march via TOUTENCOURT and LEALVILLERS to Bn. Hqd. 10th. SHERWOOD FORESTERS — P. 15. d. 2. 8.

6. A Coy. 2/ R.I. Regt. with the Lewis   A Coy. 10th. SHERWOOD FORS.
    B "   "   "   "   "   "   "   B "   "   "   "   "
    C "   "   "   "   "   "   "   C "   "   "   "   "
    D "   "   "   "   "   "   "   D "   "   "   "   "

2.

7. All Defence Schemes, Work Schemes, Aeroplane Photographs, Reconnaissance etc., will be most carefully taken over. Lists signed by Officers of both units will be sent to the Orderly Room by 7 a.m. on the 27th instant.

8. **Starting Point** - Rd. junction - 7. 10. 8. 9. 6.

9. Route:- TOUTENCOURT - TALMAS - ACHEUX road.

10. Copies of Marching Order by A. D. B. O. Coys. - ready by 7 a.m.

11. Men fallen to have rattling parts as 1.30 p.m.

12. All companies will be by Right of Coys. All companies will be by Right of Coys, all less mentioned as for "C".

13. ACHEUX House by Platoons at 200yds interval. The guides sent by coys. and for the M.G. coys. will meet them units at points above the Railway crossing across the road at 3 corner of ACHEUX WD. (Pt at c.q. 8.)

14. From & from lorries 22 and 6 recon lorries 29th. on 28th & by L.S. is responsible for returning the fodder of M.G. being system from the field line between 9th and 11th. It is to the L.line and to sent part there through P.B. material, together with Sevens, Small Boxes, Lamps etc. The position will only be accepted up nearly to return to do so until the Brigade unit the held at our lorry notice to move. believes the lorries named. The Bus R.C. Regt made to on the Right and the A.C. on the left upto the point the MCSN the un accepted.

"Appendix No 3.

Secret
                                                                Copy No __15__
        2nd Bn. & c. Royal Irish Regt. Order No. 4.
Ref. Trench Map.
                                                                17-5-18
1. The 2nd. R. Ir. Regt. will relieve the 1/R.M. Bn. in the front line of HAMEL Sector on night 19th/20th. May 1918.

2. The ANSON BN. will take over our present dispositions on night 19th/20th.

3. "A" Coy. 2/R.I. Regt. will relieve " " Coy. 1/R.M. - RIGHT.
   "C"   "   "   "   "   "   "   "   "   "   - LEFT.
   "B"   "   "   "   "   "   "   "   "   "   - SUPPORT.
   "D"   "   "   "   "   "   "   "   "   "   - RESERVE.

4. "A" " ANSON BN "   "   "C" " 2/R. Ir. Regt
   "B" "   "   "   "   "A" "   "
   "D" "   "   "   "   "D" "   "
   "C" "   "   "   "   "B" "   "

5. Guides 1 per platoon from 1/R.M. Bn will be at junction CHARLES AVE - RAILWAY CUTTING (Q.27.c.6.4.) at 10 pm.

6. Guides 1 per platoon from 2/R. Ir. Regt. will be at Cross Rds. Q.19.b.6.5. at 9 pm. Lt. BATES will take charge of these guides and ensure that the incoming units get correct guides.

7. H.Q. Guides for ANSON BN. will report at ANSON BN. HQ. at 5 pm.

8. Advance parties consisting of 1 Officer per coy., 1 N.C.O. per coy, 1 N.C.O per platoon, Nos. 1 of L.G. teams, Bn. Gas N.C.O, will report at H.Q. 1/R.M. Bn. at following times:— "A" Coy - 2 pm
                                "C" " - 2.15 pm
                                "B" " - 2.30 pm
                                "D" " - 2.45 pm

9. Advance parties from ANSON BN. will take over during the afternoon.

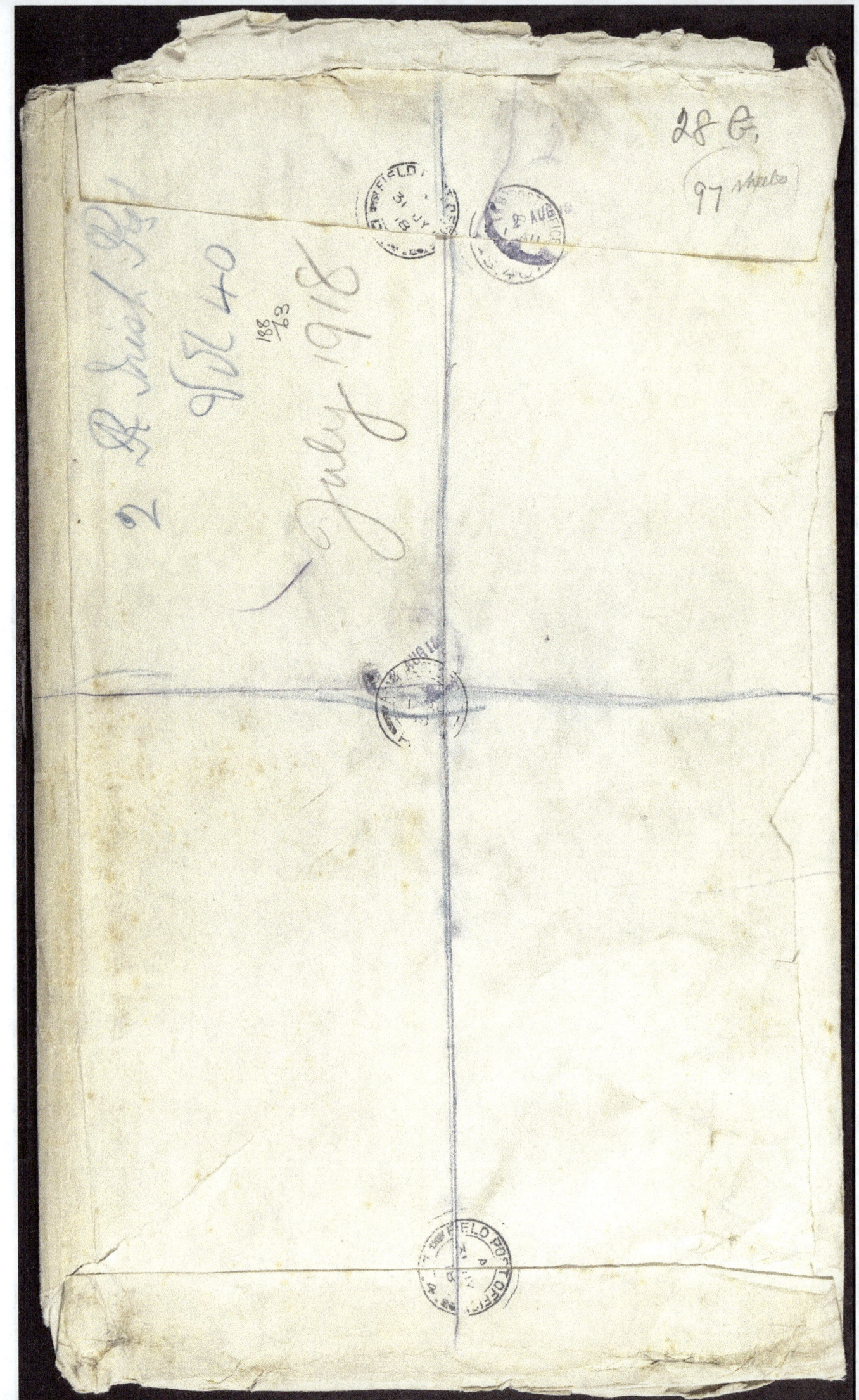

2 R Irish Rgt
9 Pl 40
188/83
July 1918

28 G.
97 sheets

Appendix No 7.

SECRET

Report on Raid
night 19/20 July carried out
by
2nd Royal Irish Regt

Army Form W.3091.

Cover for Documents.

REPORT ON RAID ON CRATER IN Q.10.b. and ADJOINING TRENCHES
by
2nd ROYAL IRISH REGIMENT - NIGHT 19th/20th JULY 1918.

Nature of Enclosures.

CONTENTS.

SECTION I   ...... GENERAL PREPARATIONS FOR RAID.
SECTION II   ...... PLAN.
SECTION III ...... EXECUTION.
SECTION IV   ...... NOTES & LESSONS.

APPENDIX "A" .... 188th INFANTRY BRIGADE ORDER.
APPENDIX "B" .... 2nd BATTALION ROYAL IRISH REGIMENT ORDER.
APPENDIX "C" .... (i) "C" COMPANY   "   "   "   ORDER.
                  (ii) "D" COMPANY   "   "   "   ORDER.
APPENDIX "D" .... 63rd (RN) DIVISION ORDER.
APPENDIX "E" .... 63rd (RN) DIVISION ARTILLERY ORDER.
APPENDIX "F" .... 188th L. T. M. BATTERY ORDER.
APPENDIX "G" .... LEFT ARTILLERY GROUP ORDER.
APPENDIX "H" .... V CORPS HEAVY ARTILLERY INSTRUCTIONS. x
APPENDIX "I" .... V CORPS COUNTER BATTERY INSTRUCTIONS. x
APPENDIX "J" .... 63rd (RN) DIVISION MACHINE GUN BATTALION ORDER.

MAP 1 .... GENERAL PLAN OF OPERATIONS.
MAP 2 .... ARTILLERY BARRAGE MAP.
MAP 3 .... MACHINE GUN BARRAGE MAP.

x Not enclosed.

Notes, or Letters written.

WAR DIARY or INTELLIGENCE SUMMARY.

Army Form C. 2118.

2 Royal Ir. Regt

(Erase heading not required.)

Place	Date	Hour	Summary of Events and Information	Remarks and references to Appendices
ACHEUX	1918. July 1		Battalion in Reserve.	See Appendix
P.15. b. a. d.	-6			No. 1. Ref. Map
P.16. a + c.				57 D.S.E.
	July 6		Battalion move into Support relieving the 7th Royal Fusiliers	See Appendix
	July 8		Battalion move into Front line relieving the 1st Royal Marine Batt. in the	See Appx. No. 2
			right post system and holding a front of 1800 yards. Dispositions of Companies	
			"B" Coy Right Coy. — "D" Coy Centre Coy. — "A" Coy Left Coy (each having two Platoons in the	
			Front line and two in Support) — "C" Coy as Support Coy.	
	July 16		"D" Coy 2nd The Royal Irish Regt. (less 6 Lewis Guns with No. 1 & 2 & 3 of Sum. Sections) is relieved	Yes. See Appendix No. 4
			in the Front Line by "A" Coy ANSON Battn. "C" Coy 2nd The Royal Irish Regt. (less 6 Lewis	
			Guns with No.s 1 & 2 & 3 of Gun Sections and personnel not taken on Raid) is relieved	
			by Rifle Sections drawn from Supporting Platoons of "A" Coy & 2nd The Royal Irish Regt. Sec relief	
			Raiding parties of "C" & "D" Coys 2nd The Royal Irish move into Brigade Reserve for Raid	
			Training.	
	July 18		"C" & "D" Coys 2nd The Royal Irish Regt. move forward and The attacking platoons vacated	See Appendix No. 5
			by Base on night of 16/17th July.	Yes.

Army Form C. 2118.

WAR DIARY
or
INTELLIGENCE SUMMARY.
(Erase heading not required.)

Instructions regarding War Diaries and Intelligence Summaries are contained in F. S. Regs., Part II. and the Staff Manual respectively. Title pages will be prepared in manuscript.

Place	Date	Hour	Summary of Events and Information	Remarks and references to Appendices
	1918. July 19	12.15	On the night 19/20th July a Raid was carried out on the Enemy's Trenches	See Appendices
	20	A.M.	the hostile raided being LEVANT TRENCH between Q.10.b.80.40 & Q.10.b.37.95 including CRATER, and LEVANT SUPPORT between Q.11.a.10.40 and Q.11.a.00.90. This raid was carried out by "C" & "D" Coys 2nd Bn. Royal Irish Regt. and proved highly successful. The attackers gained all Objectives and details of its preliminary arrangements, orders issued and full report, Notes and Lessons also congratulatory messages on the success of the enterprise.	Nos 6 & 7

Army Form C. 2118.

WAR DIARY
of
INTELLIGENCE SUMMARY.

(Erase heading not required.)

Instructions regarding War Diaries and Intelligence Summaries are contained in F. S. Regs., Part II. and the Staff Manual respectively. Title pages will be prepared in manuscript.

Place	Date	Hour	Summary of Events and Information	Remarks and references to Appendices
	1918. July 24.		Battalion is relieved by the 2nd Lincolnshire Regt. in the Rifle System and move into Billets at LEALVILLERS RAINCHEVAL spending the night en route.	See Appendix No 8.
	-25.		Billets at LEALVILLERS en route.	
RAINCHEVAL	25-27		Battalion Training.	
	28.		The 63rd (R.N.) Division is transferred from the V to the IVth Corps. Battalion moves from RAINCHEVAL to St LEGER LES AUTHIE.	
St LEGER	29.		Reconnaissance of new sector for preparation of necessary defence scheme. Battalion Training.	See Appendix No 9.
	July 1		REINFORCEMENTS OFFICERS. 2/Lt H.H. ARBUCKLE.	(M.S.)
			" R. CROFT.	
			" D. BECKETT.	
	6		Lt R.R. SPEARS.	
	7		" D.H. LLOYD.	
			2/Lt W.P. GLAVIN.	(M.S.)

Army Form C. 2118.

WAR DIARY
or
INTELLIGENCE SUMMARY.
(Erase heading not required.)

Instructions regarding War Diaries and Intelligence Summaries are contained in F. S. Regs., Part II. and the Staff Manual respectively. Title pages will be prepared in manuscript.

Place	Date	Hour	Summary of Events and Information	Remarks and references to Appendices
	1918. July 22		RE-INFORCEMENTS — OFFICERS Cont	
			2/LT M. TAYLOR.	
	24		" D BISSETT. D.C.M. M.M	
	26		" LT O.CROSBIE	
			" R. ADAMSON	
	28		2/LT W. CROFT	
			RE-INFORCEMENTS — OTHER RANKS	
	18		36 O.R.	
	23		34 "	
	26		49 "	
			DEPARTURES — OFFICERS.	
	1		2/LT F.W. BANKS.	
	20		CAPT J.P. ST JOHN PIKE. M.C. Wounded in Action	
			LT N.M. CHEEVERS "	
			CAPT. E.C. MARSH. "	

WAR DIARY
or
INTELLIGENCE SUMMARY.
(Erase heading not required.)

Army Form C. 2118.

Place	Date	Hour	Summary of Events and Information	Remarks and references to Appendices
	1918 July 10		CASUALTIES — OTHER RANKS.	
			2 O.R. Wounded in Action	
	10		2 " " " "	
	12		1 " " " "	
	13		2 " " " "	
	14		3 " Killed in Action.	
			3 " Wounded in Action.	
	15		1 " " " "	
	17		3 " Killed in Action.	
			5 " Wounded in Action.	
	19		26 " Killed in Action	
	20		3 " " " "	
			8 " Missing	

M.C. Harrison
Lieut Colonel
Commanding 2nd Nottspal Sun Rgt

SECRET.   63rd (RN) Division. No.GA.5/30.

Headquarters,
V Corps.

Duplicate
2 Copies   1 Copy sent to 3 Army with minute as below by C.C.

[Stamp: GENERAL STAFF. V CORPS. No. GX 3981 Date 25.7.18]

    Forwarded herewith full reports on a Raid carried out by two companies of the 2/Royal Irish Regiment on the night 19/20th July 1918.

    I would further remark only that as regards Section IV, para. 2 - Rate of Advance of Artillery Barrage - I consider the rate adopted to have been correct, but from verbal conversation with the raiders, and in view of para. 4 of Appendix "C" (i), and para. 4 of Appendix "C" (ii), I am inclined to think that the Raiders, on the opening of the barrage, crawled forward instead of getting up and advancing quickly till they got close up to the barrage, thereby allowing the barrage to run away from them.

(Sd) C E Lawrie

Major General,
Commanding, 63rd (RN) Division.

24th July 1918.

Third Army.

1.   This raid was made with rather inexperienced troops, and must therefore be considered a success. It was well rehearsed and I think its success was due to this.

2.   The following are points worthy of note -

  (i) Infantry do not yet make a proper and co-ordinated use of Trench Mortars and Rifle bombs. Both should have been used on the "Crater". Much more training is required.

P.T.O.

(ii)   Artillery, M.G, T.M &c Officers should always be present when Inf. rehearse raids.

(iii)   I concur in thinking that Officers expose themselves too much.   This is due, in my opinion, to Officers being content to do too much themselves instead of training N.C.Os.

(iv)   The raid was made in 2 parties and it was most necessary that the withdrawal should be simultaneous.
   This was not done and casualties resulted.
   The provisions of F.S.R, that messages must always be sent in duplicate or triplicate were disregarded, and a single message was relied upon, with disastrous results.

(v)   It is continually made evident that enemy light signals should be blocked by a smoke screen early put down.
   The value of smoke screens is not sufficiently appreciated nor is smoke sufficiently made use of.
   As in para. (i), Officers fail to make use of auxiliaries and to use any "cunning".

(vi)   "P" bombs if properly used work all right. I suspect a failure to use them in the right manner.

(vii)   Infantry must keep up to the barrage when machine guns are being dealt with.

                    (Sgd.) C. D. SHUTE, Lt.-Genl.,

                         Commanding V Corps.

26 - 7 - 18.

63rd. (RN) Division.   B.M. 1751.

A full report on the Raid carried out by the 2nd. Royal Irish Regiment on the night 19th/20th. July is forwarded herewith.
I have little to add to the remarks of the O.C., 2nd. Royal Irish Regiment in Sections III and IV attached with which I agree in general.

1. The Raid, although not as successful as had been hoped, appears to have been of value for the following reasons.

   (a) Considerable losses were inflicted on the enemy.
   (b) Identifications were procured.
   (c) Numbers of the enemy were seen running away, which must encourage not only the raiders, but all troops in the Brigade.

2. The employment of 2 Companies gave experience of what our Artillery fire, etc. is like to a considerable number of men of the Battalion, who had never been in an attack before.

3. It will be noticed that both Company Commanders employed led their men forward and were in the leading lines. In consequence one was wounded and the other lost for the time and all control vanished. While realizing their gallant conduct, I am of opinion that Commanders in a raid of this size should not be too far forward, at any rate to begin with, but should be located in some place in rear known to runners and others, where they should remain until the 1st. Objective is taken, after which they can move forward to the enemy's Front Line and re-organize for the next forward move.

4. The great value of previous rehearsals is brought out by this raid. I do not think it is too much to say that any success gained in this enterprise was largely due to these previous practices, which enabled, not only the Infantry, but also Artillery, Machine Gun and Trench Mortar Officers to form, beforehand, some appreciation of the problem in hand.

5. I do not agree with the O.C., 2nd. Royal Irish Regiment in his remarks regarding Rifle Bombs, and consider that had they been used to engage the Machine Guns encountered East of the CRATER, the Raid, very possibly, would have been completely successful.

6. The Artillery and Machine Gun arrangements appear to have been very good, and reflect, I consider, great credit on the Officers concerned in their preparation.

7. Appendices 'D' (63rd. (RN) Divisional Operation Order No. 208) and 'J' (63rd. (RN) M.G. Battn. Operation Order No. 44 with amendments) have not been attached, vide your reply to B.M. 1746 of 21/7/18 which states that these will be appended at Divisional Headquarters.

J.D. Coleridge.

22/7/18.
                                        Brigadier General,
                                            Commanding -
                                        188th. Infantry Brigade.

188th. INFANTRY BRIGADE

REPORT ON RAID ON CRATER IN Q.10.b.

and ADJOINING TRENCHES.

by

2nd. Royal Irish Regt.

Night of July 19th/20th., 1918.

SECTION I.

GENERAL PREPARATIONS.

1. **SELECTION of OBJECTIVE :-**

    (i) It had been decided by the General Officer Commanding 188th. Infantry Brigade to carry out a Raid on the enemy's lines about the 18th./19th. July with the 2nd. Royal Irish Regt.

    Three portions of the line seemed to offer opportunities for a successful Raid. These were :-

    (a) The enemy's defences in Q.10.d. - West of 'Y' Ravine.

    (b) The enemy's defences between Q.11.a.10.50. and Q.4.b.90.00. including the CRATER.

    (c) The enemy's defences between Q.4.d.97.27. and Q.5.a.33.37.

    (ii) Owing to the following objections, (a) and (c) were rejected after careful consideration.

    (a) These defences had been successfully raided by the 190th. Inf. Brigade on the night of the 4th/5th. July, when identifications had been secured and casualties inflicted upon the enemy. There was, therefore, little reason for raiding this line again so soon. As the troops holding the area had been completely surprised on the occasion of the raid, it was thought that extreme alertness would now prevail. This, coupled with the other objections, was sufficient to make a raid on this section of line undesirable.

    (c) From Patrol Reports it appeared that few, if any, men were in occupation of the trenches in front (i.e. West) of this line. The advance which it was necessary to make from our Front Line, to ensure the capture of prisoners, was, therefore, nearly 700 yards, which was considered too great a depth for a small raid. This proposal was also, therefore, rejected.

    (b) - was finally decided upon, as there had been no raid upon that section of the line for some time. There was reason to believe that the enemy occupied the CRATER and adjoining trenches at night, and the presence of suspected dugouts, Machine Gun positions etc. pointed out that there was a possibility of inflicting material damage to his defences.

/ Para. 1(iii)

Contd. - 2.

Para. 1 contd.

(iii) For the exact boundaries of the objectives chosen, see Appendix 'B' - BATTALION ORDER No. 17 - 2nd. Royal Irish Regt. and special map attached thereto.

2. PRELIMINARY CONFERENCES, ETC. :-

(i) Permission having been received to carry out the raid, on the lines indicated, the Officer Commanding and other Officers and N.C.Os. of the 2nd. Royal Irish Regiment carried out preliminary reconnaissances of the ground on 10th. July.

(ii) On July 14th. at 9-30 am. following the relief by the 2nd. Royal Irish Regt. of the 1st. Royal Marine Battalion in the line, a conference was held at Battalion Headquarters, at which the following were present :-

        188th. Infantry Brigade Commander.
        O.C., 232nd. Brigade R.F.A. (Left Group).
        O.C., 2nd. Royal Irish Regt.
        O.C., 63rd. (RN) Division Machine Gun Battalion.
        O.C., 188th. L.T.M. Battery.
        O.C., 'C' Company, 2nd. Royal Irish Regt.
        O.C., 'D' Company, 2nd. Royal Irish Regt.

(iii) As a result of this conference, the Officer Commanding 2nd. Royal Irish Regt. forwarded his proposals on the night of the 14th. July, to 188th. Infantry Brigade Headquarters.

(iv) Detailed plans based on these proposals were forwarded by the General Officer Commanding 188th. Infantry Brigade to Headquarters, 63rd. (RN) Division on 15th. July, and were approved.

(v) The General Officer Commanding 188th. Infantry Brigade held frequent conferences, after these plans had been approved, with the Officers Commanding the 2nd. Royal Irish Regiment and the units which were to support the attack.

(vi) For Orders issued by Commanders of Supporting Units see appendices of Section II. - PLAN.

3. PRELIMINARY ARTILLERY AND TRENCH MORTAR BOMBARDMENTS.

(i) Wire-Cutting.
The 232nd. Brigade R.F.A. commenced wire-cutting on 11th. July, 1918. Two 4.5" Howitzer Batteries (D/232 and D/317) were employed on this work with two 6" Newton Trench Mortars of X/63rd. T.M. Battery.
Wire was cut on the whole of the front to be raided, on the Eastern side of the CRATER and between LEVANT TRENCH and LEVANT SUPPORT.
In order not to attract special attention to the objectives, wire was also cut at the same time at Q.10.d. and Q.4.b. and d.
As the wire South and East of the CRATER could not be seen from our lines, registration on this wire was carried out with aeroplane observation.
The localities in which wire was being cut were kept under intermittent 4.5" How., 18 pdr. and Lewis Gun fire during the night, to prevent repairs being carried out.

(ii) Other Bombardments.
Known and suspected Machine Gun emplacements from which fire could be directed upon the raiding area and assembly position were bombarded systematically by 4.5" Howitzer and Trench Mortars. Special attention was paid to the localities

Contd. - 3.

Para. 3 Contd.

    (ii) - Contd.

    Q.10.b.80.80., Q.4.d.90.00., Q.4.d.90.60. Q.11.a.05.50. and Q.10.b.90.15. and the CRATER.

    (iii) For results of bombardments see Appendices 'G', 'H' and 'I' of Section III - EXECUTION.

4. **PRELIMINARY PATROLLING.**

    The enemy's wire was patrolled nightly and reports on the progress of the wire cutting was rendered each day. Patrols also constantly reconnoitred the area to secure information regarding the enemy's defences and dispositions.

5. **RELIEFS.**

    The Raiding Companies - 'C' and 'D' of the 2nd. Royal Irish Regt. were relieved by 'A' Company of the Anson Battalion in the line on the night of 16th. July, 1918. They carried out rehearsals and practices on the 17th. and 18th. and returned to the line again on the night of the 18th/19th. July. These reliefs gave an opportunity of instructing the men in the topography of the ground, in the general plan, and in the use of 'P' bombs.

6. **INSTRUCTION OF RAIDERS.**

    (i) Rehearsals.

    A taped course, on which were laid out in outline, our Front Line, the CRATER, LEVANT TRENCH and LEVANT SUPPORT, was prepared. The Raiders marched to this course on the morning of the 17th. July and the whole operation was practised.

    The Officers Commanding the 232nd. Brigade R.F.A., Left Machine Gun Group -, 63rd. (RN) Division, and 188th L.T.M. Battery were present.

    A second rehearsal was carried out on the 18th. July on similar lines and the men were instructed in the following :-

    (a) Throwing of Bombs - 'P' and Mills No. 5.

    (b) Light Signals - All the Light Signals which it was proposed to use in the attack were demonstrated several times.

    (ii) Company Commanders frequently explained to each Platoon the part it had to play.

    (iii) Special Maps and aerial photographs were also issued and explained to all Raiders.

7. **ASSEMBLY.**

    Gaps were cut in our wire just previous to the Assembly to facilitate the forming-up of our troops beyond. Tapes were laid to give the general direction of their advance to the Raiders. The Assembly Positions were also taped out.

J D Coleridge

Brigadier General,
Commanding -
188th. Inf. Brigade.

21/7/18.

SECTION II.

PLAN.

For details of PLAN see following Appendices :-

A. - 188th. Infantry Brigade Order No. 204.
B. - 2nd. Royal Irish Regt. Order No. 17.
C. - (i) 'C' Company Order.
     (ii) 'D' Company Order.
D. - 63rd. (RN) Divisional Operation Order No. 208.
E. - 63rd. (RN) Machine Gun Battalion Operation Order No. 44.
F. - 188th. L.T.M. Battery Order No. 14.

T. D. Coleridge

Brigadier General,
Commanding -
188th. Inf. Brigade.

22/7/18.

SECTION III.

EXECUTION.

1. **Forming up.**

    Raiding troops were lined out according to plan by zero minus 15 minutes. The assembly was carried out in good order and according to time table.
    Opinions differ as to whether the enemy detected the forming up; rifle and Machine Gun shots were directed towards the troops, but there were no casualties.

2. **COURSE of EVENTS.**

    Artillery and Machine Gun barrages opened punctually at Zero, synchronization being good. The general opinion of the Raiders is that the barrages were very good and accurate and well planned. Immediately the barrages commenced, the raiding troops crawled forward as near to the barrage as possible, and then rushed the enemy's Front Line directly the barrage lifted.

    Action of 'D' Company.
    It had been anticipated that a hostile Machine Gun would be found in a sap at about Q.10.b.7.3. and a special party under Sergeant FAGAN was detailed to deal with this eventuality. As expected the gun was found in position but was quickly overcome by Sergeant FAGAN's party which was skilfully handled. This obstacle cleared, LEVANT TRENCH was entered without much opposition.
    The Company then pressed on towards LEVANT SUPPORT TRENCH and met with heavy opposition from several Machine Guns East of the CRATER, between the two trenches. Only portions of 'D' Company eventually reached LEVANT SUPPORT owing to enfilade fire from about Q.10.b.85.80. Despite this, however, several dugouts were bombed. The Company was then withdrawn after a search for 'C' Company on the Left had failed, the last man to return to our lines being Captain GOWTHORPE, O.C., Company, who did excellent work in the withdrawal.

    Action of 'C' Company.
    'C' Company met with a more formidable resistance and during its advance suffered casualties from Machine Guns firing from about Q.10.b.85.80.
    The CRATER itself and the portion of LEVANT TRENCH just South of it were captured, but during this operation Captain PIKE, his Subaltern Lieut. CHIVERS, and several N.C.Os. became casualties, and from that time onwards little progress was made, and only a few men reached LEVANT SUPPORT.
    Several dugouts East of the Southern portion of the CRATER, however, were successfully bombed.
    The withdrawal of this Company was premature owing to the fact that the men mistook lights sent up by the enemy for those decided on by the Officers Commanding Raiding Companies to indicate to one another that they were ready to withdraw.
    The CRATER shewed no sign of occupation except for one bombing post about Q.10.b.70.75.; There were no signs of any attempt to open up gallery leading into our Lines.

3. **Casualties.**

    Casualties were as under :-

OFFICERS.			OTHER RANKS.			TOTAL.		
Killed.	Wounded.	Missing.	Killed.	Wounded.	Missing.	Killed.	W'ded.	Miss'g.
-	2	-	3	27	8	3	29	8

Total Casualties - 40

/para. 4.

Contd. - 2.

4. **Losses inflicted on Enemy.**

    (a) 1 Machine Gun, 4 O.Rs. captured. (2 more O.Rs. were captured but were killed on the way to our lines)

    (b) 25 O.Rs. killed - all by bombs and Rifle fire. Large numbers were seen running away, the majority of whom must have been killed by our Artillery fire.

    Numbers wounded not known.

    (c) A number of dugouts bombed.

5. **Enemy Action.**

    (a) The enemy, as usual, made use of a great number of Light Signals which were sent up directly over the area raided (but nowhere else), as soon as the Front attacked became clearly defined.

    (b) The enemy's barrage started about Zero plus 5 minutes, and lasted until our barrage ceased, when it <u>stopped almost simultaneously</u>. It was never heavy. 77 mm. shelled enemy's own wire. 150 mm. shelled South of BUFF'S AVENUE and on Right of the Brigade Sector between BEAUMONT RESERVE and the Front Line

    (c) The enemy used a number of bombs but there was very little Rifle fire, all riflemen apparently getting into dugouts directly our barrage opened and leaving the defence to Machine Gunners.

    (d) As usual, the backbone of the enemy's defence was his Machine Guns. Active guns were located as follows :-

    No. 1 at Q.10.b.78.65.   (Team killed - gun not removed)

    No. 2 at Q.10.b.83.70.   (Team - 1 killed, 1 captured, gun not removed).

    No. 3. at Q.10.b.85.80. - Silenced.

    No. 4.)   about   ) Remained in action.
    No. 5.)   Q.10.b.90.85.   )

    No. 6. at Q.10.b.7.3.   Captured by Sergeant FAGAN with team of 2 men.

    In all cases these Machine Guns were surrounded with barbed wire.

    (e) Enemy 'S.O.S' Rocket - Double Green - repeated to the rear.

21/7/18.

(Sgd.) M.C.C. HARRISON
Lieut-Colonel,
Commanding -
2nd. Battn.- Royal Irish Regiment.

SECTION III - EXECUTION (Continued.

Left Artillery Group.
(63rd. (RN) Division.)

Report on Artillery Operations connected with the Raid on night
19th./20th. July.

1. PREPARATORY. The area to be raided having been decided on on 10/7/18, wire cutting commenced on 11/7/18 and was continued daily up to the day of the raid. Two 4.5" Howitzer Batteries (D/232 and D/317) firing 106 fuzes, were employed for this, and two 6" T.Ms. of Y/63rd. T.M.B.

In order not to attract special attention to the area to be raided, wire cutting was simultaneously carried out in Q.10.d. and Q.4.b. and d.

During the same time, known and suspected M.G. emplacements from which fire could be directed on to the raiding area and jumping off place, were systematically bombarded by 4.5" Howitzers and T.Ms., special attention being paid to the localities about Q.10.b.8.8., Q.4.d.9.0., the CRATER, Q.4.d.9.6. Q.11.a.05.50. and Q.10.b.90.15.

The wire South and East of the CRATER being invisible from our Lines, both 4.5" Howitzer Batteries successfully registered it with aeroplane observation, and similarly B/232 (18 pdr. Battery) successfully registered the trench Q.4.b.90.15.

A proportion of ammunition was expended on wire cutting at night.

The Infantry Patrol reports on wire were passed to the Artillery group Commander daily and formed the basis for subsequent wire-cutting programmes.

After wire-cutting, 4.5" Howitzer and 18 pdr. fire was directed on the locality intermittently at night.

2. CONFERENCES. The Group Commander attended conferences at the H.Q. of the O.C., Raiding Battalion on 14th. and 17th.
At these Conferences, the details of Infantry and Artillery action were determined, and detailed plans were subsequently drawn up.

3. LIAISON. 2/Lieut. E.B. MORLEY, M.C., Artillery Liaison Officer with O.C., Raid, took up his duties on 14/7/18, and kept the O.C., Raid, informed as to progess in wire-cutting and passed suggestions of O.C., Raid to the Group Commander.

4. PRACTICE RAIDS. The Group Commander was present at two practice Raids carried out by the Raiding Party, and gave effect to certain minor alterations there decided on, including timing of the barrage.

5. ARTILLERY PROGRAMME. The Artillery Programme for the raid is shewn in the attached orders. The arrangements made for the raid were embodied in 63rd. (RN) Divisional Artillery Operation Order No. 208 dated 16/7/18.

Field Artillery selected for the close support of the Raid consisted of the Left Artillery Group with B/232

(1) / Battery

Contd. - 2.

Para. 5 - Contd.

B/232/ Battery of the Right Artillery Group: a total of 6- 18-pdr. Batteries and 2 4.5." How. Batteries.

The programme consisted of a creeping barrage opening on the CRATER and the German Front Line, and lifting and resting on trenches and emplacements, and finally forming the back side of a box barrage 150 to 200 yards beyond the furthest point of raid.

The sides of the Box Barrage were formed by 2 18-pdr. Batteries firing in enfilade and opening at Zero hour.

Registration was carried out with a minimum number of rounds, and two worn 18-pdr. guns were allotted tasks well over the final barrage line.

6. **HEAVY ARTILLERY.** The action of Heavy Artillery and 42nd. and 38th. Divisional Artilleries is shewn on attached plan.

7. **MAINTAINANCE OF FIRE.** The Artillery Programme was carried out as arranged, but fire was maintained until Zero plus 85, at the request of the O.C., Raid.

8. **COMMUNICATIONS.** The Liaison Officer with O.C., Raid established telephone and visual communications with Group H.Q. from the Front Line Trench and excellent communication was maintained througout the Raid.

9. **BARRAGE TABLES.** The Barrage Tables reached Battery Commanders concerned 30 hours before Zero hour, giving them ample time for preparation.

10. **MAPS.** In making preparations for a raid a good supply of flimsy maps of the raid area is of great assistance to the Artillery; Artillery Brigades have no facilities for making these maps.

(Sgd) M. TOVEY,
Lieut.- Colonel, R.F.A.
Commanding LEFT ARTILLERY GROUP,
63rd. (RN) Division.

21st. July, 1918.

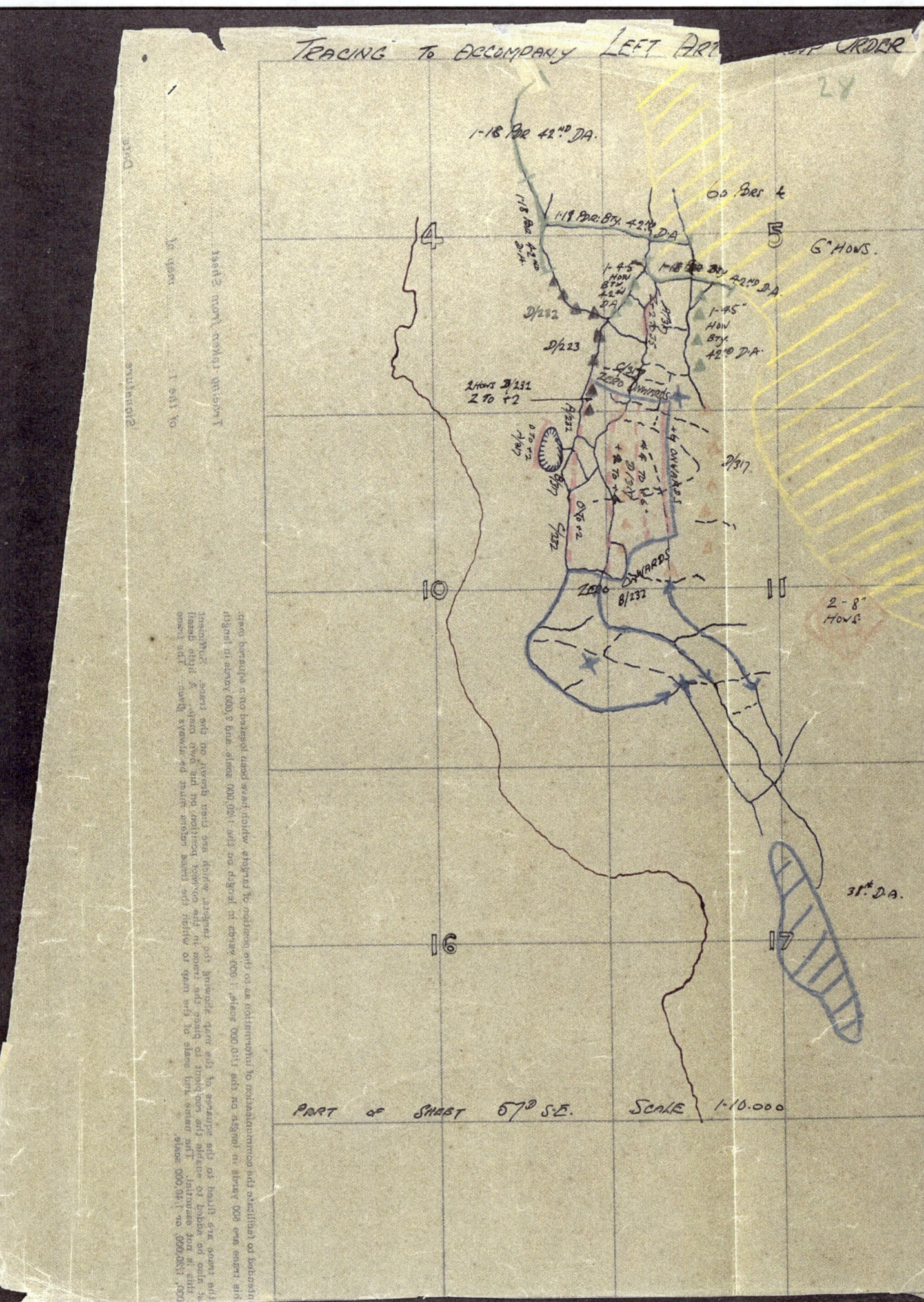

SECTION III - EXECUTION (Continued.

Report on Machine Gun Action in Raid on night of 19th/20th. July.

1. 54 Machine Guns were detailed to support the Raid. A Box Barrage was placed round the area raided, and in addition 4 guns fired direct on the Left Flank.

2. All guns opened immediately the Artillery Barrage had got well going - this was about Zero plus 10 Seconds. Fire was continued during the whole period until Zero plus 90, when, on the Signal going up, fire ceased.

3. Enemy Artillery retaliation was slight.

4. Number of rounds fired - approx. 300,000.

(Sgd.) J. LIGHTBODY,
Captain,
O.C. - Left Group - 63rd.(RN) Div.
M.G. Battalion.

21/7/18.

SECTION III - EXECUTION (Continued.

Report on Special Operations in connection with Raid by 2nd. Royal Irish Regiment on night 19th/20th. July.
---

1. **OPERATIONS.**

    2nd. Battalion Royal Irish Regt. carried out a Raid on enemy trenches on night 19th./20th.

    188th. L.T.M. Battery fired 936 rounds in support of these operations.

2. **DISPOSITION OF BATTERY.**

    1 gun was located in disused trench - at Q.10.b.1.4.

    7 guns were distributed along Bank from Q.4.c.6.7. to Q.4.c.8.5.

3. **ZERO-HOUR**

    Zero hour was 12-15 a.m.

    Trench Mortar Battery opened fire with first rounds of Artillery Barrage.

4. **TARGETS.**

    73 rounds were fired on 'Y' RAVINE at Q.10.d.6.7. with a view to taking attention from the Raiding party.

    863 rounds were fired on LEVANT TRENCH from Q.4.d.86.00. Northwards to the VALLEY and also on the Valley (Q.4.d. and Q.5.c.) Rapid fire was carried out from 12-15 am. to 12-25 am., the guns firing on the VALLEY continuing thereafter until 12-40 am.

5. **CASUALTIES.**

    1 Other Rank was wounded while serving his mortar.

6. **ENEMY FIRE.**

    Enemy retaliation was not heavy in the neighborhood of L.T.M. positions, and did not open until 3 minutes after Zero hour.

    One Machine Gun enfiladed bank (Q.4.d.) from about Q.10.d.6.7.

                                        (Sgd.) R. DONALDSON,
                                                   Lieutenant. R.N.V.R.
20/7/18.   Cmdg. - 188th. L.T.M. Battery.

SECTION IV.

NOTES and LESSONS.

1. ENEMY PREPAREDNESS.

It appears that the enemy were fully prepared for a raid on the Brigade Front, and seemed to expect it on the night it took place. From 11 p.m., when one of our Patrols approached his line, onwards, an abnormal number of Very Lights were fired along the Front; our Front Line was occasionally swept by Machine Gun and Rifle fire (an exceptional occurrence), and at one time the enemy bombed his own wire.

The forming up was quietly done, but the troops were fired on, so it is possible that movement was detected. Directly our barrage opened, the enemy sent up 2 Green Lights (S.O.S. Signal), but the hostile Artillery did not reply until Zero plus 5 minutes.

On the other hand there is no doubt that the enemy is constantly on the alert, especially as wire-cutting has been proceeding for the last week or ten days along the front, and that he has been frequently raided lately.

2. ARTILLERY and MACHINE GUN BARRAGES.

These were very good and accurate. The rate of the Infantry advance was overestimated however. In many cases our men did not keep up with the barrage and this undoubtedly enabled the enemy to get his Machine Guns in action against them and resulted in casualties. A pause was required in the first objective to re-organize the troops for an advance on to the 2nd. objective. It is thought that the pause should have been for 10 minutes, which would have meant that the Artillery barrage should have 'stood' on the 2nd. Objective to Zero plus 14 minutes before lifting.

For further details see reports of O.C., 232nd. Brigade R.F.A. and O.C. Left Group - 63rd. (RN) Machine Gun Battalion - Appendices 'G' and 'H' of Section II - Execution.

3. PLAN OF ATTACK.

Events proved that reports received from Patrols and observers were accurate. The Western edge of the CRATER was not held and was not wired. The Eastern edge, however, was well wired (the only wire on the whole front uncut) and held. For this reason a frontal attack through the CRATER would have been very difficult, as the attackers would have been obliged to climb out of the CRATER up a steep slope and through wire in face of opposition. It is thought, therefore, that the original plan of taking the CRATER from the South gave the best chances of success, and I consider it would have succeeded had not the Company Officers and N.C.Os. of 'C' Company become casualties at a critical time, and had the chain of Command after their loss been strong enough to organize attacks for the capture of the Machine Guns which held up the attack.

4. COMMUNICATIONS.

(i) The tracer ammunition used to define the flanks of the attack proved of great assistance.

(ii) It was a mistake to use Very Lights to shew that Companies had completed their tasks, as the enemy used similar lights, and in consequence, confused the raiders.

/Para. 4 (iii)

Contd.- 2.

Para. 4 - Contd.

    (iii) The bugle calls used as a guide for the raiders towards their own lines proved useful.

    (iv) The old S.O.S. Signal (Rifle Grenade bursting into 2 Red and 2 White Lights) fired at intervals of 3 minutes from our lines, to shew the raiders the way back, also proved useful ; a large supply is necessary.

    (v) Signals from Raid Headquarters rearwards worked excellently.

    (vi) The Raiding Companies took no wires with them.

    (vii) A Runner was sent back to Raid Headquarters by both Company Commanders. Neither arrived as both were wounded en route.

5. ORGANIZATION OF RAID.

The Raid, which was a large one, took place while the Battalion was in the Advanced Forward Zone, and a great deal of difficulty was found in organizing the raiding parties, before the raid, and still more in re-organizing them after their return while in the forward trenches.

To avoid these difficulties the following procedure is suggested :-

The unit selected for the raid should do a tour in the trenches, during which period the objective should be reconnoitred and 'No Man's Land' learnt by the Raiders. The Unit should then be withdrawn into Reserve when practices should take place, and then moved direct to the Front Line and carry out the Raid on the same night or day, moving through the troops holding the Front Line to do so. This done, the Raiders should move back direct to their positions in Reserve.

6. USE OF L.T.M. BATTERY.

The bulk of the L.T.M. Battery was used to thicken up the Box Barrage on the Left Flank, North of the CRATER. To judge by events, it would have been better, it appears, to have employed it against the Eastern edge of the CRATER, where its high angled fire might possibly have dealt with Machine Guns hidden behind the CRATER debris, which the field guns with their flat trajectory could not touch.

For further details see report of O.C., 188th. L.T.M. Battery - Appendix - Section II. - PLAN. EXECUTION

7. DESTRUCTION OF DUGOUTS.

The 'P' Bombs - No. 27 were not a success in destroying dugouts. They do not burn the wood-work and only make a great deal of smoke, which does not inconvenience the inhabitants provided they are not near the dugout entrance and put on their gas masks.

I consider that it would have been better to have sent over a detachment of R.E. with the Infantry, provided with special charges. This would have ensured the distruction of dugouts.

/Para. 8.

Contd. - 3.

8. **USE OF RIFLES.**

    The Raiders made very little use of rifle fire, even when numbers of the enemy were seen running away.

9. **USE OF No. 5. MILLS BOMBS.**

    A number of bombs were used for bombing dugouts and Machine Guns (in the latter case 3 times successfully. There was a certain amount of promiscuous bombing when rifle fire would have been more effective.

10. **RIFLE BOMBS.**

    These were not used. It is difficult to get accurate shooting out of these weapons by day, and this, it is considered would be accentuated at night when the position of our troops and the enemy was not properly known. Rifle Bombs might, however, prove useful if used by troops employed on flank guards.

11. **MEDICAL ARRANGEMENTS.**

    Medical arrangements were as good as could be expected. Getting the wounded down dugouts for dressing proved very difficult, and the usual difficulty of carrying men down Communication Trenches was apparent.
    Stretcher Cases took from 2 to 2½ hours to reach the Advanced Dressing Station from the Front Line.

12. **FLANK GUARDS.**

    The left flank guard did useful work and engaged hostile Machine Guns with its Lewis Guns. The right flank, after the Machine Gun at Q.10.b.7.3. was captured was not menaced ; the enemy made no attempt to leave their cover in 'Y' Ravine.

21/7/18.

21/7/18.

(sgd.) M.C.C. HARRISON,
Lieut-Colonel,
Commanding -
2nd. Battn. - Royal Irish Regiment.

Appendix 'A'

SECRET.

Copy No...........

188th. INF. BRIGADE ORDER No. 204.

Reference - Sheet 57.D. SE. - 1/20,000.

1. The 2nd. Royal Irish Regt. will carry out a raid on the enemy's trenches at an hour and on a date to be notified later, with the object of :-

    (a). Inflicting loss on the enemy.
    (b). Securing identifications.
    (c). Destroying any dugouts met with and capturing and destroying Machine Guns and Trench Mortars found in the area.
    (d). Examining CRATER and ascertaining if enemy has commenced mining therefrom.

2. OBJECTIVES :-

    <u>1st. Objective</u> :- LEVANT TRENCH between Q.10B.80.40 and Q.10.b.87.95., including CRATER.

    <u>2nd. Objective</u> :- LEVANT SUPPORT between Q.11.a. 10.40. and Q.11.a. 00.90. Patrols to be sent out as far as protective barrage admits.

3. STRENGTH of RAIDING PARTY.

    1 Officer - (O.C., Raid).
    4 other Officers, and 2 Companies (150 O.Rs.)

4. ZERO HOUR and DATE OF RAID.

    Zero Hour and Date of Raid will be notified later to all concerned.

5. ASSEMBLY :-

    The Raiding Companies will form up in front of our wire between Q.10B.5.3. and Q.10.b.4.6., being in position at Zero minus 15 minutes.

6. WITHDRAWAL :-

    There will be no recall signal. Platoons, when they have accomplished their respective tasks, will be withdrawn under orders of their own Commanders to our lines; Flank Guard Platoons being the last to withdraw.

7. DANGER POINTS :-

    The following stretches of trench in our Front Line must be avoided by raiders returning to our lines, as the fire of hostile Machine Guns will render these dangerous -

    (i) Q.10.d.2.5. to Q.10.b.2.2.
    (ii) Q.10.b.2.8. to Q.4.d.0.3.

8. ARTILLERY, TRENCH MORTAR, and MACHINE GUN SUPPORT.

    Details of these will be issued separately as Appendices, to those concerned.

Contd.- 2.

9. SIGNALS :-

   (i) The following Light Signals will be used -

   (a) A Rifle Grenade (Colour to be notified later) will be fired three times in succession from our Front Line trench, opposite the point raided, under orders to be issued by the O.C., Raid, as soon as all the raiding party have returned. On this signal the Artillery and Machine Gun Barrage will die down.

   (b) In addition, Light Signals (colour to be notified later) will be fired during the time the raid is in progress, from our Front Line, to indicate its position to the raiders.

   (ii) In addition to these Signals the following Code Words will be used :-

   (a) "PIKE" - to indicate the return of the Raiders.

   (b) "CARP" - to secure further Artillery and Machine Gun bombardment, if necessary, after the barrage has ceased.

   (iii) The Battalion Call will be sounded on the Bugle, and Rattles will be frequently sounded. These will be used to supplement the lights used to indicate the position of our line.

10. The Brigade Signal Officer will arrange to connect up the Headquarters of the O.C., Raid with the Advanced Forward Zone Battalion Headquarters by fullerphone.

11. SYNCHRONIZATION of WATCHES.:-

   Watches will be synchronized as follows :-

   (a) An Officer from each of the following will report at Brigade Headquarters for this purpose at 5-45 pm. on the day of the raid :-

   232nd. Bde. R.F.A. (Left Group)
   Left Group - 63rd. Machine Gun Battalion.

   (b) An Officer from 188th. Inf. Bde. H.Q. will report at the Headquarters of the 2nd. R. Ir. Regt. for the purpose of synchronizing watches with Officer representatives of the following units, at 7-00 pm. on the day of the raid :-

   2nd. Royal Irish Regt.
   188th. L.T.M. Battery.

12. ADMINISTRATIVE ARRANGEMENTS.

   Arrangements for escorting Prisoners, Medical Arrangements, etc., will be issued later as an appendix.

/ Para. 13.

Contd - 3.

13. O.C., 2nd. Royal Irish Regt. will forward to 188th. Inf. Bde. Headquarters, three copies of his detailed orders for the Raid, not later than 6 p.m., 18th. July, 1918.

14. ACKNOWLEDGE.

H. Steele
Captain,
A/Brigade Major,
188th. Inf. Brigade.

17/7/18.

Issued to Sigs. at 11/p.......

Copies to :-

1. File.
2. War Diary.
3. Staff Captain.
4. R.M. Battalion.
5. Anson Battalion.
6. 2/R. Irish Regt.
7. O.C., Raid.
8. No. 2 Sig. Section.
9. Left M.G. Group.
10. 188th. Inf. Bde. Transport Offr.
11. "   L.T.M.Bty.
12. 63rd. (RN) Div. 'G'.
13. "   "   "   'Q'.
14. 189th. Inf. Bde.
15. 125th. Inf. Bde.
16. 190th. Inf. Bde.
17. 249th. Fd. Coy. R.E.
18. 63rd. (RN) Div. M.G. Bn.
19. 148th. Fd. Ambulance
20. 232nd. Bde. R.F.A.

APPENDIX lv. to 188th Infantry Brigade Order No. 204.

ADMINISTRATIVE ARRANGEMENTS.

RAID IDENTITY DISCS.

Every Officer and man of the Raiding Party will be issued with duplicate red Identity Discs stamped with the Index Letter K.K. and a serial number. One of these Special Raid Identity Discs will be worn by each Officer and man in the place of the ordinary Identity Discs, which will be retained by the Battalion, the corresponding duplicate Raid Identity Disc being securely fastened thereto.

On return from the raid, the Raid Identity Disc which has been worn in the raid, will be handed back by the Officer and man in exchange for the two ordinary Identity Discs, care being taken that the corresponding raid disc is detached therefrom.

On completion of the raid the special Raid Identity Discs will be returned to Brigade Headquarters.

PRISONERS.

A special party under the supervision of an officer will be detailed for collecting prisoners and escorting them to Brigade Headquarters. It is of the utmost importance that prisoners should be sent on to Brigade Headquarters as rapidly as possible, and therefore the escorting party must be well acquainted with the best route back. All wounded prisoners, except those, who in the opinion of the M.O. are not fit to do so, will be included amongst those sent to Brigade Headquarters.

Receipts will be given for all prisoners handed over or taken over by the escorts.

The attention of all men employed on Escort duty will be drawn to G.R.Os 5823 and 3987.

MEDICAL.

An Advanced Aid Post will be established at about Q.3.d.1.3.

Relay Posts will be established in BEAUMONT

RESERVE.

The 148th Field Ambulance will be asked to supplement Battalion Stretcher Bearers. L.O. 2nd Royal Irish Regiment will arrange all details with O.C. 148th Field Ambulance.

To all recipients of 188th Inf. Brigade Order No. 204.

Appendix 'B'

SECRET.
Copy No. 3 spare

2nd. Battalion - The ROYAL IRISH REGIMENT - Order No. 17.

Ref./ Special Map attached
and 57.D. SE. - 1/20,000.

---

1. INTENTION.

   On a date and at a time to be notified later, the Battalion will carry out a raid on the CRATER and enemy trenches in the vicinity to the East and South, with the object of -

   (a) Inflicting loss on the enemy.

   (b) Securing identifications.

   (c) Destroying any dugouts met with and capturing or destroying any Machine Guns and Trench Mortars found in the area.

   (d) Examining CRATER and ascertaining if enemy has commenced mining therefrom.

   The raid will be carried out on night 19/20 July. Zero hour 12/15 am.

2. INFORMATION.

   The enemy is believed to be holding CRATER, LEVANT TRENCH and LEVANT SUPPORT. By night Machine Guns are sometimes placed in fortified shell holes in front of LEVANT TRENCH. The Eastern edge of CRATER is believed to be held. From aeroplane photographs, dugouts have been located as shewn on attached map.

3. OBJECTIVES.

   1st. Objective.
   To occupy S.W. edge of CRATER, combined with a frontal attack on LEVANT TRENCH between CRATER and Q.10.b.77.35.

   2nd. Objective.
   To penetrate enemy's position as far as LEVANT SUPPORT between Q.11.a.04.35. and Q.10.b.97.98.

   3rd. Objective.
   To attack CRATER from East and South.

4. BOUNDARIES.

   Right - Q.10.b.77.35. to Q.11.a.04.35.
   Left - Q.10.b.69.95. to Q.10.b.97.98.
   Inter-Company - Q.10.b.76.61. to Q.10.b.95.71.

5. TROOPS TO BE USED.

   'C' and 'D' Companies (strength 5 Officers and 150 O.Rs.) will carry out the raid, directly supported by -

   232nd. and 317th. R.F.A. Brigades.
   54 Guns of 63rd. (RN) Division Machine Gun Battalion.
   188th. L.T.M.Battery.
   Three 6" Newton Mortars.

   In addition, the 223rd. R.F.A. Brigade, portions of 42nd. Div. Artillery - 38th. Div. Artillery, and 42nd. Machine Gun Battalion will guard the flanks of the raid.

(1)

/Para. 6.

Contd. - 2.

6. **FORMING UP PLACE.**

   'D' Company (Right)   Q.10.b.32.32. to Q.10.b.31.47.
   'C' Company (Left)   Q.10.b.31.47. to Q.10.b.28.61.

7. **PLAN of ATTACK.**

   (a) 'D' (Right) Company will attack with 3 platoons in Front and one in close support.
   Two Sections of the Right Front Platoon will form a defensive flank in LEVANT TRENCH, attacking any Machine Gun that may open fire from shell holes on the Southern Boundary ; and one Section a defensive flank in LEVANT SUPPORT on the Southern boundary of the raid.
   Remaining two platoons (Front Line) will attack and mop up LEVANT SUPPORT without halting in LEVANT TRENCH.
   Supporting Platoon will mop up LEVANT TRENCH.

   (b) 'C' (Left) Company will attack with two Platoons in Front and two Platoons in close support.
   Right Front Platoon passing South of CRATER, without halting in LEVANT TRENCH, will attack LEVANT SUPPORT between the Company boundaries.
   Left Front Platoon to form a defensive flank, two sections to occupy Southern edge of CRATER and subsequently attack and mop up CRATER in conjunction with an attack from East by Right Support Platoon, and one Lewis Gun Section to work round Western edge of CRATER.

   Left Support Platoon, passing South of CRATER, to attack LEVANT TRENCH between Company boundaries.

   Right Support Platoon - One Section to mop up LEVANT SUPPORT and all ground between this trench and LEVANT TRENCH, Remaining two Sections passing South of CRATER, along LEVANT TRENCH, will attack CRATER from East in conjunction with attack from South by Left Front Platoon.

8. **EQUIPMENT.**

   (i) All identifications will be removed from raiders.

   (ii) Men will carry Rifles, (Bayonets fixed and dulled), 5 rounds in magazine and 1 bandolier. No other equipment.

   (iii) The Lewis Gun Sections of Platoons forming defensive flanks will each carry two Lewis Guns with 9 magazines per gun. No other Lewis Guns will be brought on raid.

   (iv) Two men per Section will carry 6 'P' Bombs No 27, each, in haversack.

   (v) Three men per Section will carry 6 Mills Bombs each in haversack.

   (vi) 2 Pairs Wire Cutters will be carried per Section. All Platoon Commanders and understudies will also carry wire cutters.

   (vii) Box Respirators will be carried by all ranks.

/ Para. 9.

Contd. - 3.

9. ARTILLERY ARRANGEMENTS.

(a) BARRAGES - Zero to Zero plus 4 minutes -
LEVANT TRENCH and CRATER (This barrage
will lift off CRATER at Zero plus 2.)

Zero plus 4 to Zero plus 7. - 1st. Lift.
(100 yards)

Zero plus 7 to Zero plus 9. - 2nd. Lift.
(100 yards)

Zero plus 9 to Zero plus 60. Form box barrage.

from Zero to Zero plus 7 minutes.

(c) 223rd. R.F.A. Brigade and portion of 38th. Division Artillery
will guard Right Flank.

(d) Portion of 42nd. Division Artillery will guard Left Flank.

(e) Corps Heavy Artillery will block enemy approaches and
shell known occupied areas.

(f) Two 6" Newton Mortars will bombard 'Y' RAVINE and
One will thicken up barrage in Valley, North of CRATER.

10. L.T.M. BATTERY.

(a) 3 guns on LEVANT TRENCH at Q.4.d.86.00.
(b) 4 guns in Valley, North of CRATER.
(c) 1 gun in 'Y' Ravine at Q.10.d.6.7.

11. MACHINE GUNS.

(a) Form a Box Barrage.
(b) Thicken barrage on Left Flank.

All Machine Guns will open fire as soon as it is obvious that
Artillery barrage has started, but not later than Zero plus 1.

12. COMMUNICATIONS.

(i) Telephone at Raid Headquarters.

(ii) If further bombardment is required, Artillery and Machine
Guns will re-open on receiving Code Word "CARP".

(iii) Complete return of raiders will be notified by :-

(a) Code word "PIKE" to all units concerned.
(b) A Light Signal, colour of which will be notified
later. The Light Signal will be a series of white asteroid
floating Lights".

(iv) (a) To guide raiders out, tracer ammunition will be
fired along flanks.

(b) 'D' Company, on completion of task allotted
will fire a series of Green Very Lights in
an Easterly direction.
'C' Company, on completion of task allotted
will fire a series of Red Very Lights in an
Easterly direction.

There will be no withdrawal until both red
and green Very Lights have been fired, when
the two Companies will retire simultaneously
under Company Commanders' orders.

with Flanks and Raid Headquarters.
2 runners will be sent to Raid H.Q. at Zero plus 40.

/Para. 13.

Contd. - 4.

13. MEDICAL ARRANGEMENTS.

   (a) An Advanced Aid Post will be established in Front Line at Q.5.b.2.1.

   (b) Relay Posts will be established in BEAUMONT RESERVE.

   (c) 148th. Field Ambulance will supplement Battalion Stretcher Bearers.

14. PRISONERS.

   Prisoners will be sent to 'B' Company Headquarters in BEAUMONT RESERVE (Q.10.c.2.7.), where they will be examined and despatched to Brigade H.Q. under arrangements to be made by O.C., 'B' Company.

15. COLLECTION of DOCUMENTS.

   2 men will be detailed from each Platoon for the collection of documents etc. found in dugouts and on dead Germans. These men will carry haversacks for this purpose, and on return will hand over what they have found to O.C., 'B' Coy. at Q.10.c.2.7. ('B' Company's H.Q.)

16. Raid Headquarters and Advanced Battalion Headquarters will be established at Q.10.b.35.50.

17. ACKNOWLEDGE.

18. DANGER POINTS
   The following stretches of trench in our Front Line must be avoided by raiders returning to our lines as the fire of hostile Machine Guns will render those dangerous :-

   (i) Q.10.d.2.5. to Q.10.b.2.2.
   (ii) Q.10.b.2.8. to Q.4.d.0.3.

19. SYNCHRONIZATION of WATCHES.

   Watches will be synchronized at Battalion Headquarters at 7-30 pm.

   Company Commanders will arrange to have at least 3 watches per Company at that hour, at Bn.H.Q. Remaining watches to be synchronized under Company arrangements.

   "   " 11)
   "   " 12. 63rd. Div. M.G. Bn.
   "   " 13.   "   "   "
   "   " 14. Anson Battalion.
   "   " 15. R.M. Battalion.
   "   " 16. Adjoining Bn. - 189th. Inf. Bde.
   "   " 17.   "   " - 125th. Inf. Bde.
   "   " 18.   Diary.
   "   " 19.   "
   "   " 20. File.

Contd. - 4.

13. MEDICAL ARRANGEMENTS.

    (a) An Advanced Aid Post will be established in Front Line at Q.5.b.2.1.

    (b) Relay Posts will be established in BEAUMONT RESERVE.

    (c) 148th. Field Ambulance will supplement Battalion Stretcher Bearers.

14. PRISONERS.

    Prisoners will be sent to 'B' Company Headquarters in BEAUMONT RESERVE (Q.10.c.2.7.), where they will be examined and despatched to Brigade H.Q. under arrangements to be made by O.C., 'B' Company.

15. COLLECTION of DOCUMENTS.

    2 men will be detailed from each Platoon for the collection of documents etc. found in dugouts and on dead Germans. These men will carry haversacks for this purpose, and on return will hand over what they have found to O.C., 'B' Coy. at Q.10.c.2.7. ('B' Company's H.Q.)

16. Raid Headquarters and Advanced Battalion Headquarters will be established at Q.10.b.35.50.

17. ACKNOWLEDGE.

M. C. C. Harrison
Lieut.- Colonel,
Cmdg. - 2nd. Royal Irish Regt.

/18.

ned at ....

tribution :-

Copy No. 1. 188th. Inf. Bde.
"   "   2.   "   "   "
"   "   3. 'A' Coy. - 2nd. R. Ir. Regt.
"   "   4. 'B'   "   "   "   "   "
"   "   5. 'C'   "   "   "   "   "
"   "   6. 'D'   "   "   "   "   "
"   "   7. 188th. L.T.M.Bty.
"   "   8.)
"   "   9.) Left Group Artillery.
"   "   10.)
"   "   11.)
"   "   12. 63rd. Div. M.G. Bn.
"   "   13.   "   "   "   "
"   "   14. Anson Battalion.
"   "   15. R.M. Battalion.
"   "   16. Adjoining Bn. - 189th. Inf. Bde.
"   "   17.   "   " - 125th. Inf. Bde.
"   "   18. Diary.
"   "   19.
"   "   20. File.

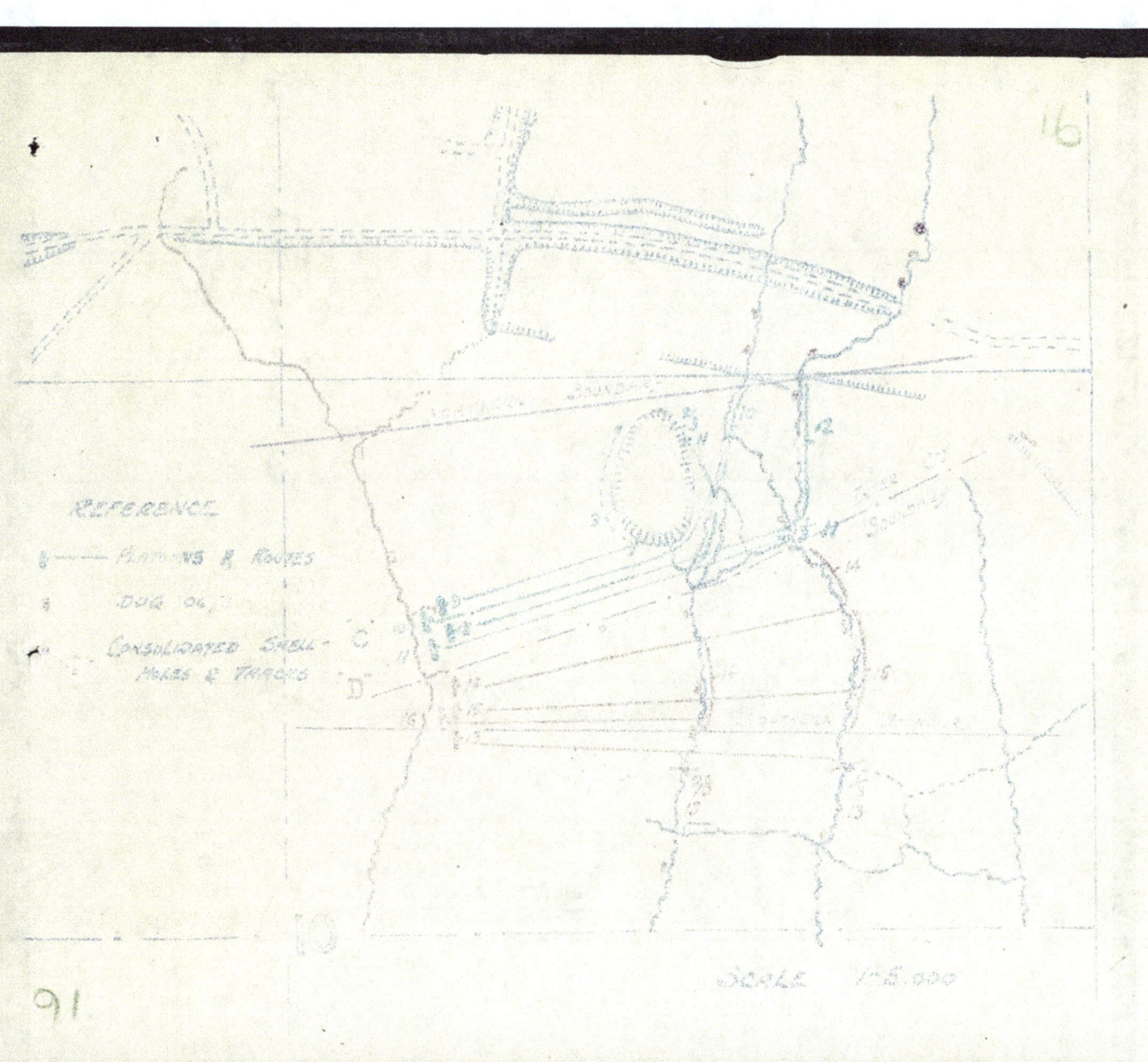

SECRET.

2nd. Battalion THE ROYAL IRISH REGT.

Appendix 'C'

Copy. No.....

Ref. Map - 57.d. SE. and special map
issued to Battn. Cmdrs.

'C' COMPANY.

SPECIAL ORDERS.

1. Issued to 'C' Company to supplement Battalion Order No. 17 dated 18/7/16 which has been read out and fully explained to all ranks concerned ; the Company, collectively and by Sections, having been brought several times over a facsimile taped course showing all objectives. Special Maps and Photographs have been issued to all Platoon Commanders.

2. DRESS and EQUIPMENT.

   (a) STEEL HELMETS (JACKETS will NOT be worn), sleeves well rolled up, BOX RESPIRATORS at the 'ALERT' position, RIFLES, 5 rounds in magazine and 1 Bandolier. BAYONETS will be dulled and shall be fixed in NO MAN'S LAND on a signal from Platoon Commander. ALL BOMBERS will wear HAVERSACKS for carrying BOMBS. The two Lewis Guns will have 9 magazines EACH. ALL Platoon Commanders and understudies and 2 men in every Section will carry WIRE CUTTERS.

   (b) Platoon Commanders will make arrangements to inspect, carefully, men's equipment etc., and personally inspect all bombs, taking care that the pins in Mills Bombs have been prepared for easy drawing.

3. ASSEMBLY.

   Platoons will be ready to move off from their respective POSTS at 9-30 p.m. and will be led by the special guides via BOWERY AVENUE to the Front Line at the points where the wire has been cut to facilitate quick assembly in NO MAN'S LAND. On a signal from O.C., Company, Platoons will be led on to the tape in front, forming up in two lines as follows :-

   No. 9 - LEFT FRONT .   No. 12 - RIGHT FRONT.
   No. 10- LEFT SUPPORT.   No. 11. - RIGHT SUPPORT.

4. ACTION of PLATOONS.

   When the Artillery Barrage commences, on a Signal from O.C., Company, all ranks will crawl forward to within a safe distance from bursting shells. When the barrage lifts, ALL will rush forward to first Objectives, Nos. 10 and 12 Platoons passing over the first Objectives and preparing for the charge to final objective , in the meantime No. 11 and two Sections of No. 9 with a Section of Lewis Guns will enter the CRATER from West and East simultaneously.

5. WITHDRAWAL.

   (a) The Signal to withdraw will be fired from the line of the final objective. A succession of RED Very Lights fired in direction of Enemy will be 'C' Company's Signal. GREEN Very Lights will be 'D' Company's Signal. The withdrawal will not commence until after BOTH those signals have been fired. All ranks to thoroughly understand this.

/ 5 (b)

Contd. - 2.

5. WITHDRAWAL - Contd.

(b) Rockets consisting of two RED and two WHITE Lights will be fired continuously from our Lines to guide all ranks back. The Bugle will sound the Regimental Call also.

(c) Nos. 10 and 12 Platoons will withdraw through Nos. 9 & 11. Care must be taken to return over the ground by which the advance was made and all casualties that may be found will be brought back to our Lines.

(d) All men returning to our Front Line will turn to the Left and pass along, proceeding (after reporting to their Platoon Commander, or understudy detailed, that they are back) along BUFFS AVENUE, and thence by Road or BOVET TRENCH to their respective localities in SUPPORT LINE.

(e) All Runners will be directed to Battalion and Company FORWARD H.Q. in FRONT LINE.

(f) STRETCHER BEARERS will be directed to the FORWARD AID POST.

(g) All men on returning to SUPPORT LINES will report at Company H.Q. to Company Clerk - L/Cpl. JAMES.

6. DOCUMENTS etc.

(a) All bodies which may be found will be stripped of identifications and documents which will be carefully brought back in SANDBAGS to O.C., 'B' Company by those specially detailed.

(b) All dugouts will be thoroughly searched for identifications and documents.

(sgd.) J. PIKE.
Captain,
O.C. 'C' Coy.

Issued at Conference of Officers
and N.C.Os. at 9-30 a.m., 19/7/18.

Copy. No. 1. - O.C., 'D' Company (Right Flank)
  "   "   2. - Col. Harrison. M.C. - Cmdg. Battalion.
  "   "   3. - "
  "   "   4. - File.

Appendix 'C 2'

S E C R E T.

SPECIAL ORDER issued to 'D' Company to supplement Battalion Order No. 17. which has been read out and fully explained to all ranks.

Ref. Map 57.d.SE. 1/20,000
and Special Map issued to all Platoon Cmdrs.

1. ZERO HOUR.
   Zero hour 12-15 a.m. - night of 19th./20th. July.

2. ASSEMBLY.

   (a) No. 13 and 14 Platoons will commence to close in at 10-30 p.m.
   No. 15 and 16 Platoons will be ready to move off from SUPPORT at 10-45 p.m. and will form up -
   No. 15 on RIGHT, No. 16 - LEFT.
   No. 13 Platoon will move off under guide to position already chosen at 11-00 p.m.
   No. 14 Platoon will move off under guide at 10-25 pm.
   No. 15 Platoon will move off under guide at 10-45 pm.
   No. 16 Platoon will move off under guide at 10-47 pm.

   (b) When marching into position, all ranks are again reminded of yesterdays conference.

   (c) At 11-30 pm. No. 13 Platoon will move into position in NO MAN'S LAND under guides already detailed.
   No. 14, 15, 16 Platoons to follow, No 13 following No. 13.
   No. 14 following No. 13.
   No. 16 following No. 14.

   (d) Disposition of Company will be :-

   No. 13 - Left. - on Right Flank of 'C' Coy.
   No. 15. Centre.
   No. 14 - Right Flank.
   No. 16 - in rear of No. 15.

3. DRESS.

   (a) Rifles with Bayonets fixed, dulled.
   (b) Box Respirators will be worn by all ranks.
   (c) Haversacks will be worn by men already detailed to carry 'P' bombs, No. 5.
   (d) All identifications will be removed. Special identification discs will be issued later.
   (e) Platoon Commanders will inspect Men's equipment & bombs.

4. SIGNAL for ADVANCE.

   Platoon Commanders will note barrage, and must be careful that they do not get too close. All ranks are reminded of yesterdays conference.

5. PLAN of ATTACK.

   No. 13 Platoon on LEFT. One Section on Left must keep in touch with 'C' Coy. At final Objective two Sections will mop up.

   No. 14 Platoon. At 1st. Objective one Section and Lewis Gun Section will form a defensive flank in LEVANT TRENCH.
   At final Objective No. 14 Platoon will form defensive flank in LEVANT SUPPORT.

   (1).   /5. (Contd.)

Continued - 2.

5. Plan of Attack - Contd.

No. 15 Platoon in centre. At final Objective will mop up.

No. 16 Platoon will form up in rear of No. 15, and will not advance to final Objective but will mop up. LEVANT TRENCH as already detailed.

6. DOCUMENTS etc.

(a) All bodies which may be found will be stripped of identifications and documents which will be carefully brought back in sandbags to O.C., 'B' Company by those specially detailed.

(b) All dugouts will be thoroughly searched for identifications and documents.

7. PRISONERS.

Prisoners will be sent down BUFFS AVENUE to 'B' Coy. H.Q.

8. SIGNAL for RETURN.

(a) 'C' Company will fire a series of RED Lights on completion of their work.
Each Platoon on their completion of their task will inform Company Headquarters in LEVANT SUPPORT.
As soon as all tasks have been completed 'D' Company Signal will be a series of GREEN lights.
The order to return will be sent to Platoons by runner.

(b) Rifle Grenades bursting into two RED and two WHITE lights will be fired from our Lines to give direction.
A bugle will sound the Regimental Call.

9. WITHDRAWAL.

(a) Care will be taken to return over the same ground and all casualties that may be found will be brought back to our Lines.

(b) After returning to our lines, all men will proceed to Company H.Q. via BUFFS AVENUE and along BEAUMONT RESERVE and report to 2nd. Lieut. COADY.

(c) All runners and Stretcher Bearers will be directed to Battalion and Company Headquarters Aid Post.

Issued at 2-00 p.m.　　　　　(Sgd.) R.W. GOWTHORPE, Capt.
　　10/7/18.　　　　　　　　　　　　O.C. - 'D' Company.

Copy No. 1. O.C. - 'C' Coy.
 "   " 2. Commanding Officer.
 "   " 3.
 "   " 4. File.

APPENDIX 'D'

SECRET.   Copy No. 22

Ref:- Trench Map 1/10,000.
Part of 57d. S.E.

63rd (RN) DIVISION ORDER No. 249.

RAID.
1. The 188th Infantry Brigade will carry out a Raid on the night 19th/20th July 1918 with the object of -

    (a) Capturing and killing Germans - as many prisoners to be taken as possible.

    (b) Obtaining identifications and documents.

    (c) Capturing Machine Guns and destroying dug-outs.

2. **OBJECTIVES.**

    (a) **1st Objective.** "LAVANT TRENCH", from Q.10.b.8.4. to Q.10.b.87.95., including Crater.

    (b) **2nd Objective.** Q.11.a.1.4., to Q.11.a.0.9.

3. **Strength of Raiding Party.** 5 Officers and 150 O.R.

4. **ZERO HOUR.** (The hour at which the Artillery bombardment will open) will be fixed by the 188th Infantry Brigade and notified to Divisional Headquarters by 10.0 am. on the 19th July, by whom it will be communicated to all concerned.

5. **Artillery Support.** The C.R.A. will arrange -

    (a) To cut the necessary wire before the date of the raid. Wire on other parts of the Divisional front to be cut at the same time.

    (b) For the requisite Field and Heavy Artillery support. (A copy of the Artillery programme to be forwarded to Divisional Headquarters).

6. **Machine Gun Support.** The Officer Commanding 63rd Machine Gun Battalion will (in consultation with the C.R.A.) arrange for the Machine Gun Support required. (A Copy of Machine Gun programme to be forwarded to Divisional Headquarters).

7. **Light Signals.**

A WHITE asteroid rocket, bursting into a single floating star will be fired three times in succession from our Front Line trench opposite the point raided, under orders to be issued by O.C. Raid, as soon as all the Raiding Party have returned.
In addition, Rifle Grenades, bursting into two RED and two WHITE stars will be fired during the time the raid is in progress commencing from ZERO plus 20 minutes from our Front Line to indicate its position to the raiders.

8. **Synchronization of Watches.**

    (a) A General Staff Officer from Divisional Headquarters will synchronize the watches of the undermentioned at their respective Headquarters at the following hours on the 19th July:-

        C.R.A. .... 5.0 pm.
        63rd M.G.Battn. .... 5.30 pm.
        188th Inf. Bde. .... 5.45 pm.

(b) The C.R.A. will arrange for the synchronization of watches of the Heavy Artillery and flanking Artilleries taking part in the raid.

9. ACKNOWLEDGE.

J. H. Soutry

Lieutenant Colonel,
General Staff,
63rd (RN) Division.

15th July 1918.

Issued to Signals at:- 11.0. pm.

DISTRIBUTION:-

Copy No. 1.   O.O.File.
        2.- 3. War Diary.
        4.- 6. A.A. & Q.M.G.
        7.   63rd Div. Arty.
        8.   63rd Div. Engrs.
        9.   188th Inf. Bde.
        10.   189th Inf. Bde.
        11.   190th Inf. Bde.
        12.   63rd M.G.Battn.
        13-14. V Corps.
        15.   V Corps H.A.
        16.   V Corps R.A.

SECRET.   63rd (RN) Division. No.GA.5/30/5.

A.A. & Q.M.G.
63rd Div. Arty.
63rd Div. Engrs.
188th Inf. Bde.
189th Inf. Bde.
190th Inf. Bde.
63rd M.G.Battn.
V Corps.
V Corps H.A.
V Corps R.A.

1.   Reference para.4 of 63rd (RN) Division Order No.249.

     ZERO Hour will be 12.15 AM on 20th July, 1918.

2.   ACKNOWLEDGE.

                                              Major General,
19th July, 1918.   Commanding 63rd(RN) Division.

Appendix 'E'

SECRET.

63RD (R.N.) DIVISIONAL ARTILLERY OPERATION ORDER No.208.

Headquarters R.A.,
16th July 1918.

1. The 188th Inf.Brigade will carry out a raid on the enemy trenches on the night 19th/20th July 1918.
FIRST OBJECTIVE. LAVANT Trench from Q.10.b.8.4. to Q.10.b.8.7., including the CRATER.

SECOND OBJECTIVE. Q.11.a.1.4. to Q.11.a.0.9.

2. The 63rd (R.N.) Divisional Artillery, together with 42nd and 38th D.A's. and V Corps Heavy Artillery, will co-operate according to Table and map attached.
The C.B.S.O. has also arranged a Counter Battery programme. "Silent" guns will take part.

3. Sufficient ammunition will be dumped beforehand at the guns so that at the end of the operation the normal amount is still on the positions.

4. Artillery Brigade Commanders will please arrange that the nature and extent of hostile Artillery action is recorded and reported to these H.Q. as soon as possible.

5. ZERO HOUR will be notified later.

6. Synchronization of watches will be arranged by Divisional Artillery Signal Officer.

7. At Zero plus 60' [35' crossed out], fire will cease. Batteries will, however, remain on the line of their last tasks in case of need, until instructed from these H.Q. to resume normal "S.O.S." lines.

8. Wire cutting by the Field Artillery covering the Battalion front is being carried out continuously.
The Group Commander concerned will obtain the assurance of the Infantry that the wire has been cut to their satisfaction prior to the raid.

9. No mention of this operation is to be made on the telephone.

10. ACKNOWLEDGE.

G.C. Walford
Major R.A.,
Brigade Major,
63rd (R.N.) Divisional Artillery.

Copies to -
R.A. V Corps.
C.B.S.O., V Corps.
42nd D.A.,
95rd Bde.R.G.A.
188th Inf.Bde.
190th Inf.Bde.
223rd Bde.R.F.A.,
63rd (R.N.) D.A.C.,
O.i/c.Sigs., 63rd D.A.
Rec.Officer,
File.

H.A. V Corps,
63rd (R.N.) Divn.
38th D.A.,
63rd Bn.M.G.C.,
189th Inf.Bde.,
317th Bde.R.F.A.,
232nd Army Bde.R.F.A.,
63rd (R.N.) D.T.M.O.,
Staff Captain,
War Diary,

33RD (R.W.) DIV.ARTY.TASKS.
(To accompany 33rd D.A.Operation Order No.208)

TIME.	UNIT.	TASK.	RATE.	AMMN.	REMARKS.
"	"	"	"	"	"
"	"	"	"	"	"
"	"	"	"	"	"
ZERO to Z + 2'.	A/317.	Bombard CRATER from Q.10.b.70.96.— Q.10.b.65.70.	"Rapid".	T.S.	50% on graze.
ZERO to Z + 4'.	A/232.	Bombard from Q.4.d.88.20.to Q.10.b.80.85.	"	"	" See (3 guns on the line of the first shoots (lift, i.e. Q.5.c.10.10.— 2 & 3. (Q.11.a.02.85.
"	B/317.	Bombard from Q.10.b.80.85.to Q.10.b.80.50.	"	"	" (3 guns on the line of the first (lift, Q.11.a.02.85.—Q.11.a.02.50.
"	C/232.	Bombard from Q.10.b.80.50.to Q.90.b.80.15.	"	"	" (3 guns on the line of the first (lift, Q.11.a.02.50.—Q.11.a.00.15.
ZERO onwards.	C/317.	Bombard from Q.4.d.90.20.along NEW BEAUMONT Rd.to Q.5.c.40.05.	"	"	Forms North side of Box barrage.
ZERO onwards.	B/232.	Bombard from Q.10.b.80.15.to Q.10.b.95.14.thence along trench running Easterly to Q.11.a.38.30.	"	"	Forms South side of Box Barrage.
ZERO to Z + 4'.	D/317.	Bombard the line from Q.11.a.10.99.— Q.11.a.10.25.	"	"	H.E.Delay.
Z + 4' to Z + 7'.	"	Lift 100 yards.	"	"	
Z + 7' to Z + 60'.	"	Bombard the line Q.5.c.60.10.to Q.11.a.50.40.to Q.11.a.40.10.	"Normal".	"	
ZERO onwards.	D/232. 4 hows.	Bombard front line from Q.4.d.70.75.—Q.4.d.99.50.— Q.4.d.90.30.	"Rapid" for first 3 mins.then Normal.	H.E.105 fuze. & delay	105 fuze will not be fired S.of Q.4.d.99.50.
ZERO to Z + 5'.	D/232. 2 hows.	Bombard LEVANT Trench at Q.4.d.85.00.	"Rapid".	H.E.delay.	At Z + 5' + 2 hows switch N.to front line at Q.4.d.90.30.

Contd........

1.

Sheet 2.   63RD (R.H.) DIV.ARTY.TASKS.

TIME.	UNIT.	TASK.	RATE.	AMMN.	REMARKS.
ZERO onwards.	D/223.	Superimposed on task of 4 Hows.of D/232.			
ZERO onwards.	RIGHT GROUP less D/223.	(a) Bombard front line from Q.10.d.75.99. to Q.11.c.35.40. (b) Trench from Q.10.d.99.99. to Q.11.c.66.45. (c) Trench from Q.11.c.40.99. to Q.11.c.90.55.	"Rapid" for first 6 mins. then "Normal".	50% T.S. 50% "AX".	
Z + 2' to Z + 60'.	A/317.	Lift and switch on to trench Q.5.c.50.75.—Q.5.c.25.40.	"Normal".	T.S.	
Z + 4' to Z + 7'.		Barrage the line Q.5.c.10.10.—Q.11.a.02.85.			1st lift of 100 yds.
Z + 7' to Z + 9'.	A/252.	Barrage the line Q.5.c.30.05.—Q.11.a.22.85.	"Normal".	T.S.	2nd lift of 100 yds.
Z + 9' to Z + 30'.		Bombard the line Q.5.c.40.10.—Q.11.a.35.85.			3rd lift forming part of E. side of Box Barrage.
Z + 4' to Z + 7'.		Barrage the line Q.11.a.02.85.—Q.11.a.02.50.			1st lift of 100 yds.
Z + 7' to Z + 9'.	(B/317.	Barrage the line Q.11.a.22.85.—Q.11.a.20.50.	"Normal".	T.S.	2nd lift of 100 yds.
Z + 9' to Z + 60'.		Bombard the line Q.11.a.35.85.—Q.11.a.35.50.			3rd lift forming part of E.side of Box Barrage.

contd..........

2.

Shoot 5.

TIME.	UNIT.	TASK.	RATE.	AMN.	REMARKS.
Z + 4'to Z + 7'.		Barrage the line Q.11.a.02.50.— Q.11.a.00.15.	"Normal".	50% T.S.	1st lift of 100 yds.
Z + 7'to Z + 9'.	C/252.	Barrage the line Q.11.a.20.50— Q.11.a.20.30.			2nd lift of 100 yds.
Z + 9'to Z + 60'.		Bombard from Q.11.a.35.50.to Q.11.a.35.30.			3rd lift forming part of E. side of Box Barrage.

63RD (R.N.) DIV.ARTY.TASKS.

42ND DIV. ARTY. TASKS.
(To accompany 63rd D.A. Operation Order No.208)

TIME.	NATURE.	TASK.	RATE.	AMN.	REMARKS.
	1-18 Pr. Bty.	Bombard front line from Q.4.b.70.97.-Q.4.b.55.35.		50% T.S. 50% "A"	After Zero + 6 half the guns of each Battery were turned and back in angular lifts as far as LINSEED SUPPORT on Q.5.a.
ZERO onwards	-do-	From Q.4.b.55.35.-Q.4.d.66.80.	Z to Z + 6':- "Rapid". Z + 6' onwards: "Normal".	SMOKE	
	-do-	Enfilade LIVE ALLEY from Q.4.b.65.15.-Q.5.a.49.05.		50% T.S. 50% AX	
	-do-	Enfilade LINSEED LANE from Q.5.c.25.90.-Q.5.c.80.77.			
	1-4.5" How. Bty.	Bombard LINSEED RESERVE from Q.5.c.55.80.-Q.5.c.50.20.	"Normal".	H.E. 106 fuze.	
	1-4.5" How. Bty.	Bombard from Q.5.c.30.85.-Q.5.c.05.	"	"	

38TH (WELSH) DIV. ARTY. TASKS.
(To accompany 63rd D.A. Operation Order No. 208.)

TIME.	UNIT.	TASK.	RATE.	AMM.	REMARKS.
ZERO to Z + 35'. 60	3-18 pr. Batteries.	Bombard trenches from Q.17.a.95.60.–Q.17.d.35.55.	Z to Z + 6' :- "Rapid". Z + 6' onwards:- "Normal".	50% "A". 50% "AX".	
Zero to Z+60	1 - 4.5" Howitzer Battery.	make screen from Q.17.a.10.95 – Q.17.a.75.90.			

HEAVY ARTILLERY TASKS.

(To accompany 63rd Div.Arty.Operation Order No.208)

TIME.	TASK.	NATURE.
ZERO to 60'.	Bombard Trench systems in Q.5.a. Trench Junction at Q.5.c.80.80. Sunken Roads and Banks in Q.5.d., Q.11.a & b.	} 6" Howrs. and 60 pdrs.
ZERO + 35'.	STATION Road at Q.11.d.35.85.	8" Howrs.
	As shown in traxing attached.	

6" TRENCH MORTARS.

ZERO to 35'.	Bombard	Q.10.d.95.65. Q.11.c.50.50. Q.5.c.45.40. Q.5.c.35.80.	"Rapid" first 6 mins. then "Normal."

****

APPENDIX 'F'.

188th. L.T.M. BATTERY - ORDER No. 14.

1. **OPERATIONS.**

    The 2nd. Battalion Royal Irish Regt. will carry out a Raid on enemy trenches on night 19/20th. July, 1918.

    188th. L.T.M. Battery will carry out a special firing programme in support of these operations.

    Zero hour will be 12-15 am.

2. **DISPOSITION of T.M. BATTERY.**

    Battery will consist of two Sections.

    (a) <u>No. 1 Section</u>. (Sub.-Lieut. J.A. BEDFORD, R.N.V.R.)
        1 Gun located in disused trench - (Q.10.b.1.4.)

    (b) <u>No. 2 Section</u>. (2/Lieut. W.H. BROWNE)
        7 Guns distributed along bank from Q.4.c.6.7. to)
        Q.4.c.8.5.)

    (c) <u>BATTERY HEADQUARTERS</u> (during operations) will be at Q.4.c.7.6.

3. **TARGETS.**

    (a) <u>No. 1 Section</u> - One gun will fire on 'Y' RAVINE at Q.10.d.6.7 making a demonstration at commencement of operations to take attention from raiding party.

    (b) <u>No. 2 Section</u>.- Three guns will fire on LEVANT TRENCH from Q.4.d.86.00. - northwards to VALLEY.
        Four guns will fire on VALLEY (Q.4.d. and Q.5.c.) fire to be continued until Signal is received that Raiding Party has returned.

4. **RATE of FIRE.**

    (a) <u>No. 1 Section</u>.

        No. 1 Gun. - Zero to Zero plus 4 - 20 rounds per minute.

    (b) <u>No. 2 Section</u>.

        All Guns. - Zero to Zero plus 10 - 20 rds. per minute.
        Nos. 2,3,4, & 5 " - Zero plus 10 to Zero plus 30)
        5 rounds per minute)

5. **LIGHT SIGNALS.**

    (a) Rifle grenades bursting into two red and two white lights will be sent up during operations to shew raiders direction of line.

    (b) Red and Green Very Lights will be sent up by Companies on completion of allotted tasks.

    (c) White asteroid floating lights will be sent up when all the raiding party has returned.

(1)

/Para. 6.

Contd. - 2.

6. COMMUNICATION.

    Communication between Sections and Battery Headquarters and between Battery and Battalion Headquarters will be maintained by runners.

7. REPORTS.

    Reports (Ammunition,- Expenditure, Casualties etc.) will be rendered to Battery Headquarters at 4-00 am.

8. "S.O.S" GUNS.

    "S.O.S" Guns will be brought from BEAUMONT RESERVE to Advanced Battle Positions after "Stand to" on 19th. inst.
    They will be retained in these positions until after "Stand to" on 20th. inst. when they will be again set up in emplacements in BEAUMONT RESERVE.

9. PLEASE ACKNOWLEDGE.

18/7/18.
       (Sgd.) R. DONALDSON,
         Lieut. R.N.V.R.,
     Cmdg. - 188th. L.T.M. Battery.

APPENDIX 'G'.

SECRET   Copy No. 13.

LEFT ARTILLERY GROUP
63rd (RN) DIVISION.   18th July, 1918.

With reference to 63rd (RN) Divisional Artillery Operation Order No. 208, a copy of which with plan on scale 1/10,000 showing Artillery barrage is forwarded to all batteries.

1. In the opening barrage for A/232, B/317 and C/232 Batteries, half the guns will open on the German front line as shown in Sheet 1 of the Table of Tasks, and half will open on the Second line, i.e. at a lift of 100 yards, these latter guns remaining on this line from Zero to Zero plus 7, the whole lifting together at Zero plus 7.

2. In the event of any gun being considered insufficiently reliable for close shooting, it will, from the first fire 200 yards beyond the final barrage line.
   Batteries will report by 12 noon, 19-7-18, the number of guns so dealt with.

3. Artillery fire will continue until Zero plus 60 minutes unless orders to cease firing are received from Group H.Q.
   The order to cease firing will be sent by the code work "PIKE".
   The order to re-open fire, if necessary, will be sent by the code word "CARP". On receipt of this order, Batteries will re-open on their tasks for the final box barrage at rate - one round per gun per minute.

4. In the event of the S.O.S. Signal going up on the Group front before Zero minus 30 minutes, S.O.S. fire will be opened.
   Between Zero minus 30 and Zero S.O.S. fire will not be opened unless ordered by Group H.Q.
   If the S.O.S. Signal goes up between Zero and Zero plus 60 minutes, batteries will continue their programme for the raid.

5. Batteries will ensure that correctors are calculated sufficiently long to give 50% on graze. Only ammunition in good condition to be used, and it is to be sorted as carefully as possible.

6. 2/Lieut. E.B.MORLEY, MC. (C/232) is detailed as Artillery Liaison Officer with the O.C.Raid. Separate instructions have been issued to him.
   2/Lieut. A.P.HALL, (C/317) is detailed as understudy to 2/Lieut. E.B.MORLEY.
   2/Lieut. E.B.MORLEY will report in wiring to Group H.Q. by 9 am. 20th instant.

7. The Group F.O.O. on duty on the night 19th/20th will be in direct communication with Group H.Q. between Zero minus 15 mins. and Zero plus 60 minutes; between these hours telephone lines in advance of Group H.Q. will be used for tactical messages only.

8. F.O.O. and Batteries will immediately report to Group H.Q. the nature and extent of any hostile fire.

                                          Sd. E.A.BINNEY, Capt.R.F.A.
                                     Adjutant, Left Artillery Group,
                                              63rd (RN) Division.

APPENDIX 'J'.

SECRET   Copy No. 1.

63rd (RN) MACHINE GUN BATTALION OPERATION ORDER No.44.

Ref.Map 57/D, S.E. 1/20,000.

1. On the night 19th/20th July the 188th Infantry Brigade will raid the trenches marked Red in attached tracing.

2. The following M.G. units will co-operate :-

    12 guns.   42nd Battalion, M.G.C.
    10 guns.   'C' Company.)
    8 guns.   'A' Company.) 63rd (RN) M.G. Battalion.
    6 guns.   'B' Company.)
    8 guns.   'D' Company.) (Reserve).
    8 guns.   38th Battalion, M.G.C.
    ----
    54 guns.

3. The above will have tasks as follows :-

Battery Position.	Guns.	Time.	Target.	Rate of fire.	Remarks.
'A' Battery to be selected by OC.42nd M.G. Battalion.MGC.	8	Zero to 'cease fire' signal.	Q.4.b.25.75. to Q.4.b.25.95. searching 500 yds.East.	100 R.P.M. for first 5 mins. 75 R.P.M. for next 30 mins. 100 R.P.M. from Zero plus 35 to 'Cease fire' signal.	Found by 42nd Bn. M.G.C.
'B' Battery. to be selected by OC.42nd Bn. M.G.C.	4	-do-	Q.5.a.21.00. to Q.5.a.28.40.	-do-	-do-
'C' Battery. Q.3.a.85.45.	4	-do-	Q.4.b.05.63. to Q.4.b.25.65. searching 500 yds.East.	-do-	Found by 'C' Co.63rd M.G. Bn. M.G.C.
'D' Battery. Q.9.b.6.4.	6	-do-	Q.4.d.50.88. to Q.5.c.00.45.	-do-	(1) Guns will be laid direct. (2) Found by 'A' Co.
'E' Battery. Q.2.d.75.70.	6	-do-	Q.4.d.36.28. to Q.4.d.44.50. Enfilading Rd. 500 yds.	100 R.P.M. for first 5 mins. 75 R.P.M.for next 30 mins. 100 R.P.M. from Zero plus 35 to 'Cease fire' signal.	(1) Guns will be ld.direct. (2) Found by 2 guns 'A'Co. 2 guns 'C'Co. 2 guns 21st M.G.Bn.

-2-

Battery postion.	Guns.	Time.	Target.	Rate of fire.	Remarks.
'F' Battery. Q.3.d.8.6.	2	Zero to 'cease fire' signal.	~~xxxxxxxx~~ enfilade N. side of bank Q.11.a.10.99.	100 RPM.for first 5 mins. 75 R.P.M.for next 30 mins. 100 RPM.from Zero plus 35 to 'cease fire' signal.	(1) Guns will be laid direct. (2) Found by 'C'Co.
'G' Battery. Q.4.d.05.74.	2	Zero to Zero plus 5	Trench Q.10.b.85.95.	125 R.P.M.	(1) Guns will be laid direct. (2) Found by 'C'Co
'H' Battery. Q.25.a.0.94.	4	-do-	1st Task. Q.11.a.25.20. to Q.11.a.45.20. Searching N. 400 yards.	125 R.P.M.	Found by 'B' Co.
-do-		Zero plus 7 to 'Cease fire'signal.	2nd Task. Q.5.c.3.0. to Q.5.c.5.0. Searching N. 500 yards.	75 R.P.M.to Zero plus 35 then 100 RPM to 'cease fire' signal.	-do-
'I' Battery. Q.15.a.55.80.	6	As for 'A'Bty.	Q.10.d.62.55. to Q.10.d.50.85. Searching 450 yds. N.E.	As for 'A' Battery.	Found by 21st M.G.Battalion.
'J' Battery. To be selected by OC.38th M.G.Bn. MGC.	4	-do-	Q.11.a.95.60. to Q.11.a.75.65. Searching 250 yds.N.E.	-do-	Found by 38th M.G.Battalion.
'K' Battery.to be selected by OC.38th MG.Bn.	4	-do-	Q.11.a.95.05. to Q.11.d.2.9.	-do-	-do-
'L' Battery. Q.15.b.6.1.	4	-do-	Q.11.c.37.60. to Q.11.c.25.80. Searching 350 yards.	-do-	Found by 'B' Co. 63rd M.G.Bn.

4. If the situation is clear at 10 minutes after the 'Cease fire' Signal Batteries will be withdrawn under unit arrangements.

5. The Left Group Commander is responsible for all detail M.G. arrangements and safety precautions. He will arrange with the Brigade Major 188th Infantry Brigade to clear any trench in the danger area.

6. Battery positions will be prepared on the night previous to the raid and all guns will be in position by Zero minus 2 hours.

7. Sufficient belted ammunition for requirements will be carried in and the empties will be returned to Rear H.Qs. for refilling immediately after cease fire. Under no circumstances will reserves be depleted.

8. Orders as to synchronization of watches will be issued later. A Runner will be despatched to H.Q. of Units mentioned in Para.2 at 5.30 pm. on the 19th July.

P.T.O.

9. M.G.Companies, 38th Battalion, M.G.C. and 42nd Battalion M.G.C. to acknowledge.

                                    Sd. T.R.McCREADY, Lt.Col.RM.
                       Commanding 63rd (RN) M.G.Battalion.

Issued at Midnight.
   15th/16th July.

*****

Identification Trace for use with Artillery Maps.

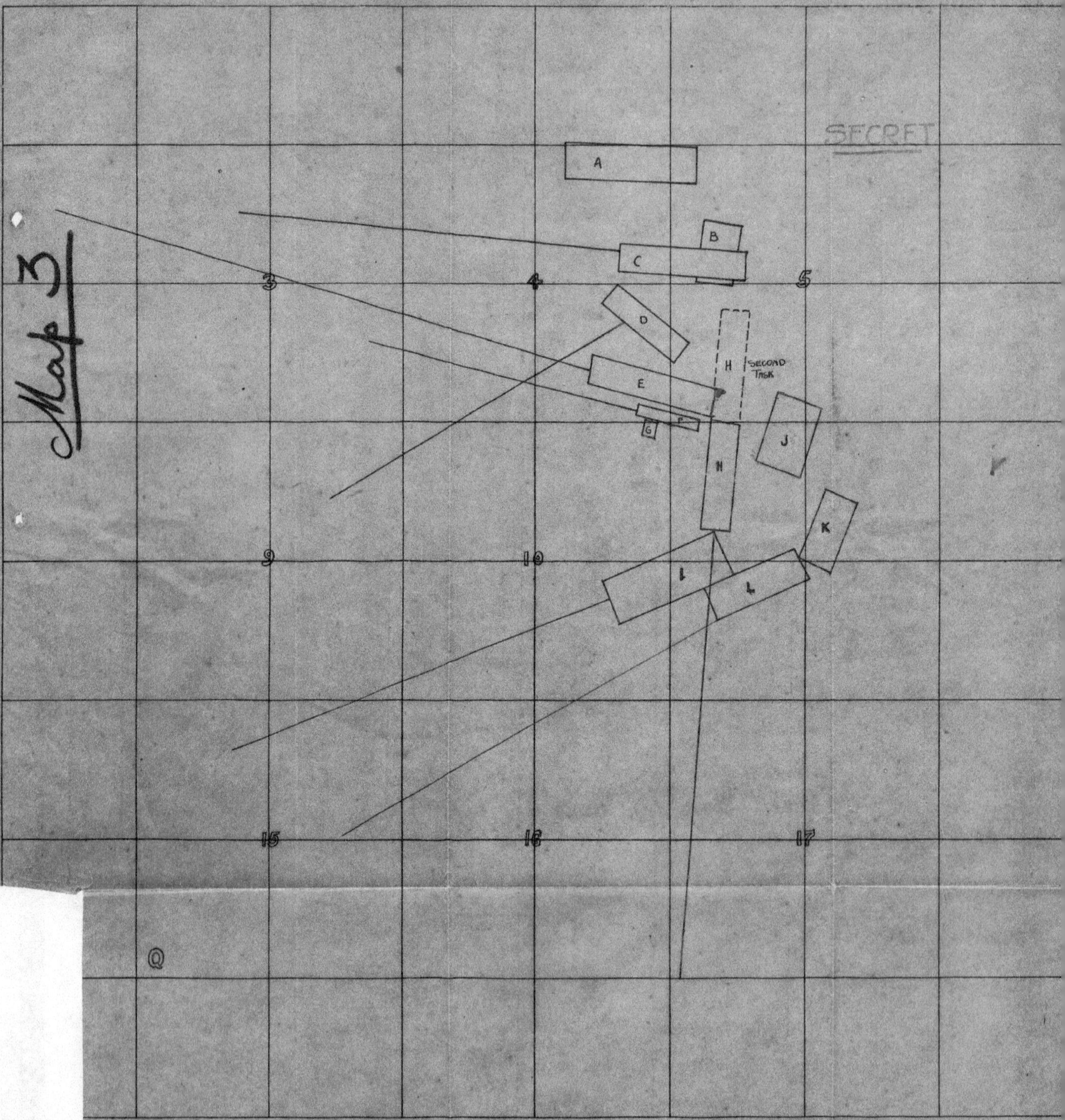

Map 3

SECRET

Tracing taken from Sheet 57a S.E.

of the 1: 10,000 map of

MAP 1.

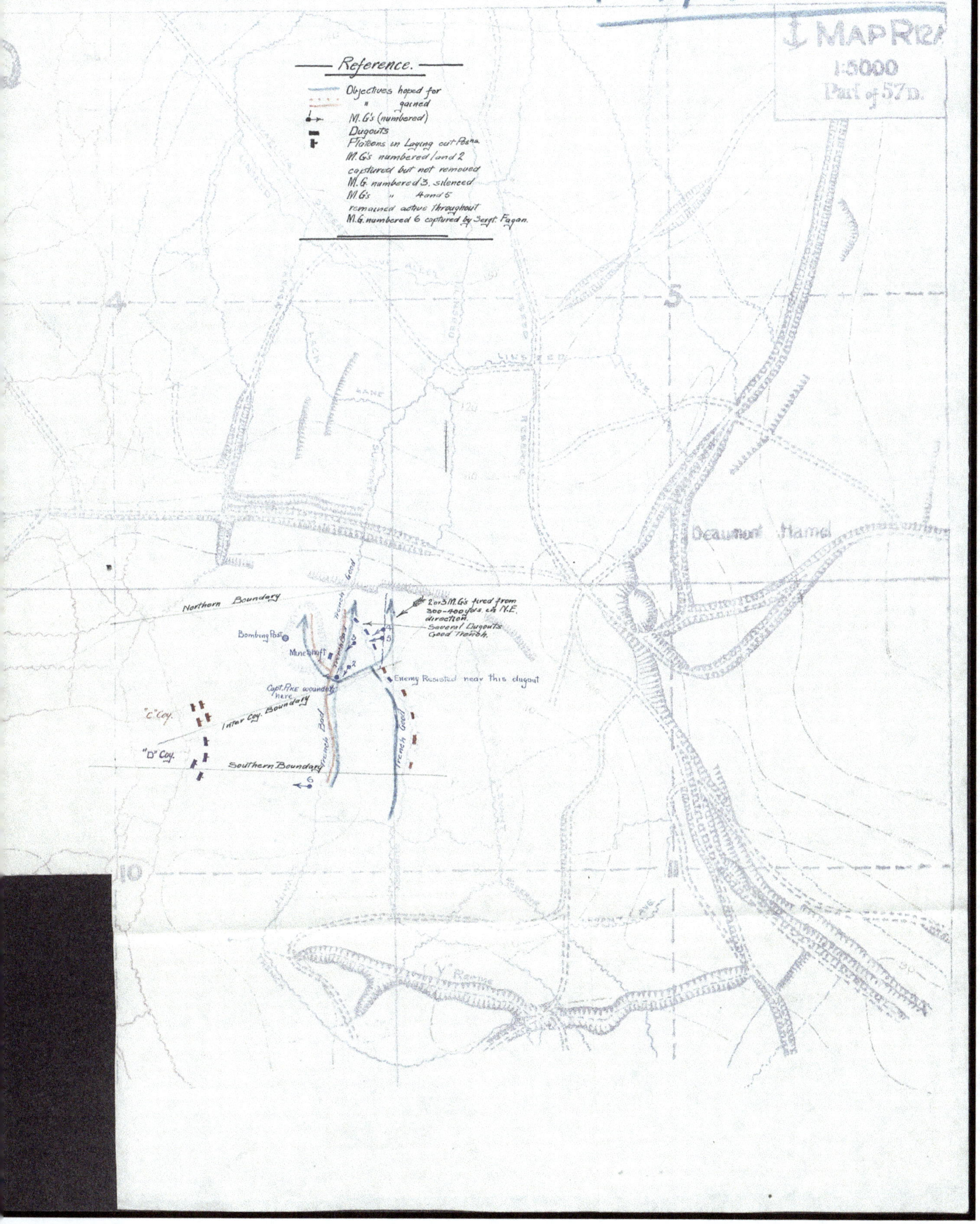

MAP RI2
1:5000
Part of 57D.
Reference.
Objectives hoped for
" gained
M.G's (numbered)
Dugouts
Platoons in Laying out Posns.
M.G's numbered 1 and 2
captured but not removed
M.G. numbered 3. silenced
M.G's " 4 and 5
remained active throughout
M.G. numbered 6 captured by Sergt. Fagan.
4
5
Beaumont Hamel
Northern Boundary
Trench Good
2 or 3 M.G's fired from
300-400 yds. in N.E.
direction.
Several Dugouts
Good Trench.
Bombing Post
Mineshaft
Trench Bad
Enemy Resisted near this dugout
Capt. Pike wounded
here
"C" Coy.
Inter Coy. Boundary
"D" Coy.
Southern Boundary
Trench Bad
Trench Good
10
"Y" Ravine

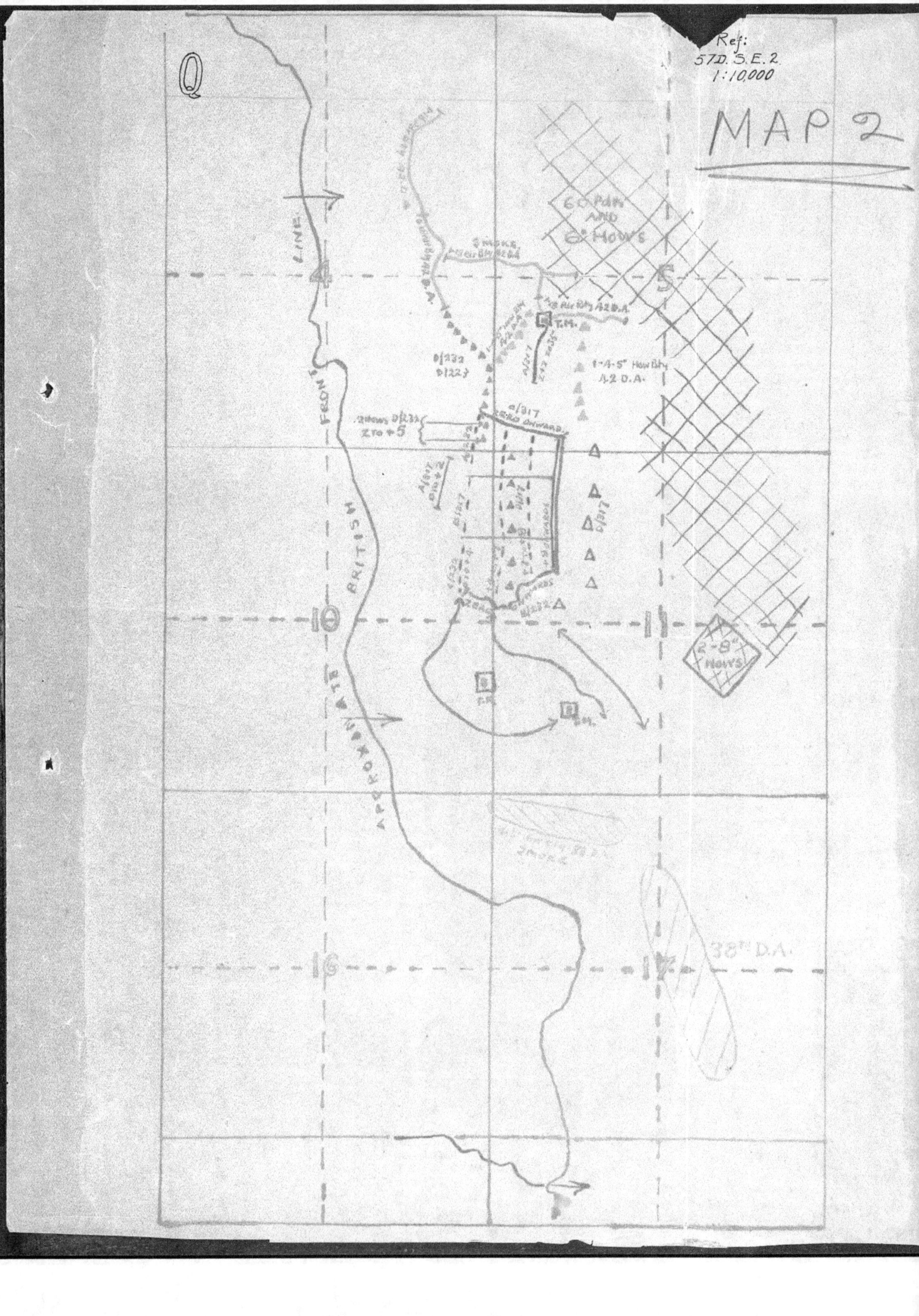

Ref:
57D. S.E. 2
1:10,000
MAP 2
Q
60 PDR AND 6" HOWS
4
5
10
11
16
17
T.M.
1-4.5" How Bty 42 D.A.
2 HOWS D/232 Z TO +5
D/317
2-8" HOWS
BRITISH FRONT LINE
APPROXIMATE
38th D.A.

Appendix No 2

Secret   2nd Bn. R. Irish Regt   No. ...   Copy No 15
R.F. 5y C Sta 1/3000   In Field, 5th July 1918

1. The 18th Inf. Bde. will relieve the 190th Inf. Bde. in the Left Sector of the Divisional Front on the night 6th/7th 1918. The 2/R. Regt. will relieve the 2/R.I. Rif. in Support.
   "A" Coy. 2/R.I. Reg. will relieve A Coy 2/R.I. Rif.
   "B"   "   "   "   B   "   "   "
   "C"   "   "   "   C   "   "   "
   "D"   "   "   "   D   "   "   "

2. On relief 2/R.I. Rif. will occupy accommodation vacated by 2/R.I. Regt.

3. All defences and work schemes, aeroplane photographs, trench maps and trench stores books &c carefully handed and taken over — Lists to reach Orderly Room by 9 a.m. 7th July 1918.

4. The instructions contained in (?...?) Div. Trench Standing Orders will be complied with.

5. Intervals of 200x between Platoons will be maintained when moving in the open.

6. Advance parties consisting of 1 Officer per coy, 1 N.C.O. per Coy, 1 N.C.O. per platoon, 1 N.C.O. for Bombers, & 1 N.C.O. (Signallers) to report at HQrs. of units they are relieving at 6 p.m.

   1 N.C.O. and 3 men to take over guards on ammunition dumps will accompany "A" Coy's advance party.

7. The 2/R.I. Rif. will supply guides — 1 per platoon

2

and 1 for Coy. HQrs. at C.y.d.6.4. at 10 p.m. Two guides for Bn.HQrs. will be at level crossing C.1.d.45.40. at 10.15 p.m.

8. Relief complete to Bn.HQrs. by code word HÉRISSART.

9. An advance party from 7/R.I. Fus. will arrive at Bn. HQrs. about 6 p.m. Guides - 1 per platoon from 7/R.I. Fus. will arrive during the afternoon and return to Support Bn. after tea.

10. Officers' kits to be stacked at Bn.HQrs. @ 6 p.m.

11. 1 Mess Cart, 1 Maltese Cart and 1 Limber to be at Bn. HQrs. at 8 p.m.

1 L.G. limber to be at each Coy. HQrs. at 8 p.m. to carry cooking utensils, Spare L.G. S.A.A., water tins filled & officers' trench kits.

J.V. O'Reilly
Capt. & Adjt.,
2nd. R.I. Insk. Regt.

Issued at 10 p.m.
Copies to
No.1. HQ 188 Bde.
2. O/C 7/R.F.
3. Sec-in-Cmd.
4. O/C A Coy
5. " B Coy
6. " C Coy
7. " D Coy

No. 9. Q.M.
10. I.O.
11. R.S.M.
12. Sig. Sgt.
13. Cook Sgt.
14. Diie
15. War Diary
16. Spare.

Secret 2nd Bn The Royal Irish Regt Orders No. 31 Copy No. 15

Ref 57 D. SE 1/20,000.   "The field" 12.7.1918

1. The 2/Royal Irish Regt will relieve the Royal Marine Bn. in the night front system on the night 13/14th July 1918.

"A" Coy 2/Royal Irish will relieve left support Coy of R.M. Battn.
"B"   "   "   "   "   right front Coy   "   "   "
"C"   "   "   "   "   left front Coy   "   "   "
"D"   "   "   "   "   Centre   "   "   "

"B" Coy will move off at 10 pm via AUCHONVILLERS and BUFFS AVENUE.

"D" Coy will move off via BOVET and BUFFS AVENUE after "B" Coy leaving at 10.30 pm.

"C" Coy will move off via BOVET TRENCH and BOWERY AVENUE leaving at 10 pm.

"A" Coy will follow "C" Coy leaving at 10.30 pm.

Bn Hd Qrs will move off at 10.30 pm.

2. The usual advance parties consisting of 1 OFFICER and 1 NCO and Gas NCO per Coy and 1 NCO per platoon, Lewis Gunners, Signallers (Coy and Bn Hd Qrs) and Bn Gas NCO will move off at 5 pm to take over.

This advance party will furnish necessary guides for remainder of Company. Places to be selected by Coy Commanders.

3. All Trench Stores, Defence Schemes, Work Schemes, Dispositions, Maps and Aeroplane Photographs will be carefully handed and taken over and Trench Store Lists will be forwarded to Orderly Room by 9 am 14th inst.

4. Completion of relief will be reported to Bn Hd Qrs by code word "DUCK".

5. Transport — 1 limber per Coy to be at Coy ration dumps at 10 pm. 1 limber, Maltese and mess cart to be at Bn Hd Qrs at 10 pm.

                                    Captain a/Adjt
                                    Royal Irish Regiment
                                              over

Issued at   am.
Copies to.
1.   188th Bde H.Q.   9. M.O.
2.   O/c Rn Battn   10. Q.M.
3.   Sec. in command.   11. T.O
4.   O/c "A" Coy   12. R.S.M.
5.   O/c "B" Coy   13. Sigs Sgt
6.   O/c "C" Coy   14. Cook Sgt
7.   O/c "D" Coy   15. Res Diary
8.   Int. Officer.   16. File

War Diary

Appendix to No 4. / No 8

2/1st Regt. Operation Order No 32.

The Field 16.7.18

1. A Coy ANSON Bn. will relieve D Coy. 2/1st Regt. in the advanced Forward Zone tonight.

   A Coy 2/1st Regt. will detail 1 full rank N.C.O. and 1 rifle section from each of the supporting platoons to take over the 2 posts of C Coy in TITAN AVE.

   O/C A Coy. will also detail an Officer to live at present C Coy HQ & take over command of 2 posts in TITAN AVE and TITAN S.1.

   The remaining posts at present occupied by C Coy will not be held.

2. On completion of relief the raiding parties of C & D Coys. will move to Bde. Reserve & come under the orders of the O/C ANSON Bn. for tactical purposes.

3. Guides (per. platoon) & usual advanced party from D Coy. will report at Coy HQ. A Coy ANSON Bn. at 6 p.m. this evening.

   Trench stores, defence schemes, etc to be carefully taken over. Receipts forwarded to this office by 11 a.m. 17th inst.

   Guides will conduct ANSON Bn A Coy to posts at present occupied by D Coy. On completion of relief these guides will conduct their own platoons to localities vacated by A Coy ANSON Bn.

   Advance party of C Coy. will report

at Point "ANSON" Pn (Q.7.d.8.5.) at 6 pm
1 guide per platoon will return to present
dispositions to conduct C Coy to quarters
vacated by O.C. ANSON Bn, on completion
of relief by A Coy

4. A & B Coys will each leave the following
on present dispositions –
  6 L.Gs with Nos 1 & 2
  1 Cook & cooking utensils
C Coy take away all empty petrol tins
D Coy hand over —— " —— " ——

5. Rations. D Coy. 29 rations & all full
water tins to be brought up in ANSON
A Coy limber. Remaining rations of
D Coy to be sent to present A Coy
ANSON Bn ration dump.
  C Coy rations & all full petrol tins
to be sent up on C Scot. Bn H.Q.
limber. Remaining rations of C Coy
to be sent to ANSON Bn H.Q. Ration
Dump.

                                    [signature]
                                    Capt & Adjt
                                    7 R.I. Regt.

Copies
1 O/C ANSON Bn   6 O/C D
2 2ic R.F.   7 O.C. A
3 O/C A   8 War Diary
4 O/C B
5 O/C C

Appendix No 5.

O.O No 10
By
Lt Col H&C Harrison M.C.
Comm'd 2 Royal Irish Regiment
18/7/18.

INTENTION 1) A Coy Anson Bn in the advanced Forward zone will be relieved tonight 18/7/18 by "B" Coy 2RI Regt. "D" Coys 2R I Regt Nos 1 & 2 + other details at present with "A" Coy Anson Bn will stand fast

2) "C" Coy 2RI Regt will re-occupy position vacated by them on night of 16/17/7/18. On arrival of "C" Coy 2RI Regt the two sections from "A" Coy 2RI Regt will immediately rejoin their Coy.

3) "D" Coy 2RI Regt will relieve via "Buffs" Av.
"C" Coy will come up via Bowry Av.

4) Coys will move off by Platoon

at 200ˣ interval.
5) "D" Coy R1 Regt will move
off at 10.15 pm
"A" Coy will move off with
first Platoon 200ˣ after "D"
Coy last platoon.

Guides Will not be required

Advanced Party OC "D" Coy will detail
one officer, 1 NCO &
one NCO per platoon to take over
trench stores etc. French Stores
etc. will be reported correct or
otherwise dept to OR by 10 am
19/7/18. This party will be at
A Coy Hqrs Anson Bn at 8 pm

Transport One limber will report
to "O C "C" & "D" Coy at
A Coy Hqrs Anson Bn @
10 pm to bring up Cooking
Utensils, empty Water Tins, Officers
Revd Kits to Dump used at present
by Bn Hqrs R1 Regt.

All ration limbers will come
up tonight as before. the night
of 16/17 the late C.O.s will arrive & to be by tonight
~~Km...~~ ~~...~~
~~of from...~~

Completion of Relief will be notified
to Bn Hqrs R I Regt
by C & S Coys ???

Code Word — "Butter" —

Rickmer Ridge

Issue of O 4.15 pm
1 copy to OC A Coy R Regt
 "   "   "   Linden Bn
 "   "   C Coy (detail) R I Regt
        C & S Coys
 "   OC Queen Bn
 "   GH & TO R I Regt

                    A.G. Butler

Appendix No. 6.

SECRET.

63rd. (RN) Division.   B.M. 1565.

1. I propose carrying out a raid with the 2nd. R. Irish Regt. about the night of 18th./19th. July.

2. I originally intended to raid enemy's lines from about Q.4.d.50.35. to about Q.4.b.60.27. but from patrol reports received this morning - vide 188th. Inf. Bde. Intelligence Summary No. 3 of to-day - it would appear that there are few, if any, Germans occupying this area. As I consider an advance to the line Q.4.d.95.27. to Q.5.a.33.37. somewhat deep for a small raid, I am inclined to think that a raid on the enemy's defences between Q.11.a.10.50. and Q.4.d.90.00. (including CRATER) would be more satisfactory, especially as there is reason to believe that the enemy occupies the CRATER and the adjoining trenches by night.

3. Before sending in detailed plans, I am particularly anxious that the 2nd. R. Irish Regt (and especially the raiders) should have an opportunity of reconnoitring the ground to enable the O.C. Battalion to draw up his scheme, which will be forwarded to you at the earliest opportunity.

4. I have informed the O.C., Artillery Group of the probable point on which the raid will take place, and wire is being cut along the whole Brigade front.

5. The front to be raided is about 250 yards. I consider, therefore, that 2 small Companies of about 80 O.Rs. each should be employed ; 1½ Companies actually raiding and ½ a Company kept in hand for eventualities. It may be advisable, however, to raid other portions of the enemy's lines simultaneously, to draw attention from the main point of attack, in which case the half Company referred to above will be used and possibly other troops brought up to act as Reserve.

6. In the meantime every effort is being made to obtain an identification by means of battle patrols, but the enemy is extremely wary and seldom occupies the same positions two nights running.

J. D. Coleridge

Brigadier General,
Commanding -
188th. Inf. Brigade.

9/7/18.

Copies to :-

    2/R. Irish Regt.
    317th. Bde. R.F.A.
    63rd. M.G. Battalion

OR 663

O.C. "D" Coy.

For information, please.

J. O'Reilly Capt.
2nd R. Irish.

10/7/18

SECRET.   N. 980.

To:- All Batteries & Detd. Sections (317th. Bde.)
         etc...
         Inf. Bde.
         ----

1.   The 2nd. R. Irish Regt. propose to carry out a raid on the night 18th./19th. July.

2.   Most probable point between Q.11.a.10.50. and Q.4.d.90.00. (including CRATER)

3.   D/317 will expend 100 rounds a day wire cutting between these points.
     The remainder of their allotment will be used for the systematic destruction of T.Ms.
     N. 968 dated 9/7/18 is cancelled (for D/317)

4.   D/232 will expend 100 rds. of their daily allotment cutting wire in Q.4.b. and d. and between Q.10.d.80.35. and Q.10.d.62.50.

5.   T.Ms. will expend 40 rds daily cutting wire in front and North and South of the Crater.

                              (Sgd.) H.T.LIPLAND (?)
                                     Captain R.F.A.
                                     Adjutant,
10/7/18.   317th. Brigade R.F.A.

2/R. Ir. Regt.   - 2 -   B.M. 1600.

                    For information.

                                     R H Campbell
                                     Captain,
                                     for Brigade Major,
                                     188th. Inf. Brigade.
11/7/18.

Proposals for raid on CRATER in Q.10.b.

1. **Objective and General Plan**: To penetrate enemy's position as far as LEVANT SUPPORT between Q.11.a.1.4 and Q.11.a.0.9. Attack CRATER from SOUTH in conjunction with frontal attack on LEVANT TRENCH.

2. (a) C and D Coys. approximate strength 5 Offrs. and 150 O.R. will carry out the raid. The two flank coys. holding our front line will each take over one of the centre boats in the front line at present held by D Coy.
All available trench mortars, machine guns and artillery will be used.

(b) C and D Coys. will form up in front of our wire between Q.10.b.6.5.3. and Q.10.b.4.6. Start leaving front line trench at zero — minus 30'.

(c) Tasks. C Coy. left front platoon to enter Southern end of CRATER and proceed at once to Northern end to form a defensive flank. Left support platoon in close support to above to mop up CRATER.
Right front Platoon - objective LEVANT SUPPORT from Q.10.b.95.75. to Northern boundary. Right support

3.

All troops of left Coy in front line will engage any hostile M.G. that may open fire on our raiding party from North of NEW BEAUMONT ROAD.

Advanced Coy and Bn. HQrs at Q.10.b.3.6.

3. Artillery arrangements:
(a) Artillery will be required to cut wire all along Battalion front previous to night of raid.
(b) Barrage.   Zero to Zero + 2' - LEVANT TRENCH including CRATER
Zero + 2' - Zero + 4'   -   Lifts 100ˣ
Zero + 4' - Zero + 6'   -   Lifts 100ˣ
After Zero + 6'   -   Box barrage (see map)

Two howitzers will fire on LEVANT TRENCH where trench crosses grid line immediately North of CRATER from Zero to Zero + 5' - Valley North of CRATER to be heavily engaged.

4. (a) Zero hour 12 midnight or 1.30 am.
(b) Telephone wires to be laid to advanced H.Q. - Artillery to be stopped by code word "PIKE" and rockets (colours to be notified later).

4

(c) Advanced Aid Post at Advanced Bn. HQrs - relay posts in BEAUMONT RESERVE

(d) Prisoners to be sent to D Coys HQrs where they will be carefully examined and searched and handed over to an escort supplied by B Coy. They will then be conducted to Bde. HQrs.

(e) Men will carry rifles and fixed bayonets - 5 rds in magazine and wear one bandolier to the equipment.

L.G: - 9 magazines per gun
2 men per section carry 6 "P" bombs each in haversack.
3 men per section carry 6 Mills bombs per man in haversack
2 pr. of wire cutters per section to be carried

5. M.G barrage (n. of guns to be settled later).

Zero +1' - Zero + 5' - LEVANT SUPPORT in Q.11.a. from Q.16.d
Zero +1' - Zero + 5' - 2 guns on LEVANT SUPPORT where trench crosses grid line North of CRATER

5

Valley North of CRATER continuously
Also Zero + 5' M.Gs in Q.16.d.
Left on 'G' LINSEED SUPPORT
LINSEED TRENCH is divided
between Artillery and M.Gs see
attached map.

6 Stokes Mortars:
   3 on LEVANT TRENCH N. of CRATER
   4 on Valley
   1 on Y RAVINE

14-7-18. M C C Harrison Lieut Colonel
Commanding 2nd Bn The R... Regt

2

platoon LEVANT TRENCH from
Q.10.b.85.65 to Northern Boundary
excluding all works between this trench
and water CRATER.

D Coy will attack with 3 platoons
in front and 1 in close support.

Two sections of right platoon
will form a defensive flank in LEVANT
TRENCH and 1 section a defensive
flank in LEVANT SUPPORT at Southern
Boundary.   Remaining two platoons
in front line will attack and mop
up LEVANT SUPPORT without halting
at LEVANT TRENCH.

Supporting platoon will mop up
LEVANT TRENCH.

Dividing line between Coys Q.10.b.94.5
to Q.10.b.95.75 — D Coy taking the
communication trench.

The L.G. sections with left front
platoon of C Coy and right front
platoon of D Coy will each bring
2 L.G. guns. Remaining platoons
will not carry L. Guns.

As troops of left these L Gs will
take up positions at Northern End of
CRATER and at Southern boundary of
LEVANT TRENCH.

63rd Division. No. G.A. 5/30.

V CORPS.

G.X. 3981.
26th JULY 1918.

THIRD ARMY.

1. This raid was made with rather inexperienced troops, and must therefore be considered a success. It was well rehearsed and I think its success was due to this.

2. The following are points worthy of note -

(i) Infantry do not yet make a proper and co-ordinated use of Trench Mortars and Rifle bombs. Both should have been used on the "Crater". Much more training is required.

(ii) Artillery, M.G., T.M., &c. Officers should always be present when Infantry rehearse raids.

(iii) I concur in thinking that Officers expose themselves too much. This is due, in my opinion, to Officers being content to do too much themselves instead of training N.C.Os.

(iv) The raid was made in 2 parties and it was most necessary that the withdrawal should be simultaneous. This was not done, and casualties resulted. The provisions of F.S.R. that messages must always be sent in duplicate or triplicate were disregarded, and a single message was relied upon, with disastrous results.

(v) It is continually made evident that enemy light signals should be blocked by a smoke screen early put down. The value of smoke screens is not sufficiently appreciated nor is smoke sufficiently made use of. As in para. (i) Officers fail to make use of auxiliaries and to use any "cunning".

(vi) "P" Bombs if properly used work all right. I suspect a failure to use them in the right manner.

(vii) Infantry must keep up to the barrage when machine guns are being dealt with.

(Sgd) C. D. SHUTE,
Lieutenant General,
Commanding, V Corps.

26th July 1918.

Third Army No. G.12/293.

O.O.C., V CORPS.

Reference your G.X. 3981 dated 25/7/1918.

I agree with your remarks and consider the raid very satisfactory and the lessons learnt to be of the greatest value.

28/7/1918.   (Sgd) J. BYNG, General.

-2-

V CORPS.
G.X. 3981.

63rd DIVISION.   28th July 1918.

Please see attached remarks by Army Commander and Corps Commander on raid carried out by 2nd Royal Irish Regiment on night 19th/20th July.

(Sgd) T. V. LEAHY, for
B. G., G. S.,
V CORPS.

-3-

63rd (RN) Division. No. GA. 5/30.

188th INFANTRY BRIGADE.

Forwarded for information.

Lieutenant Colonel,
General Staff,
63rd (RN) Division.

30th July 1918.

S E C R E T.   Copy No 6

Detailed Plan for Raid on CRATER in Q.10.b. and adjoining trenches

(vide Map and attached tracings   Reference Maps :-
                                                  57.D. SE. 1/20,000
                                                    "   "   1/10,000
1.   OBJECTIVE and GENERAL PLAN.   Tracings 'A', 'B', & 'C'

   1st. Objective. - To attack CRATER from the South, combined
   with a frontal attack on LEVANT TRENCH between
   Q.10.b.80.40. and Q.10.b.87.95.

   2nd. Objective - To penetrate enemy's position as far as
   LEVANT SUPPORT between Q.11.a.1.4. and Q.11.a.0.9., and
   to send out Patrols as far as protective barrage admits.

   Objects of Raid.

   (a) To inflict loss on the enemy.
   (b) To secure identifications
   (c) To destroy any dugouts met with, and to capture and
       destroy any Machine Guns and Trench Mortars found
       in the area.
   (d) To examine CRATER and ascertain if enemy has commenced
       mining therefrom.

2. (a) TROOPS TO BE USED.

   (i)   8 Officers and 2 Companies ('C' and 'D' Companies - about
         150 O.Rs.), 2nd. Royal Irish Regt.
   (ii) The 232nd. and 317th. R.F.A. Brigades.
   (iii) The 63rd. (RN) Div. Machine Gun Battalion.
   (iv) The 188th. L.T.M. Battery.
   (v)   3 6" Newton Mortars.

         In addition to the 223rd. R.F.A. Brigade, and portions of
         the 42nd. Division Artillery, 38th. Div. Artillery,
         and 42nd. Machine Gun Battalion will guard the flanks of
         the raid.

(b) FORMING UP PLACES.

         The raiding Companies will form up in front of our
         wire between Q.10.b.5.3. and Q.10.b.4.6., and will be
         in position by Zero minus 15 minutes.

(c) TASKS - FORMATIONS - MOPPING-UP PARTIES.

   (i) 'D' (Right) Company will attack with 3 Platoons in front
        and one in Close Support.
        Two Sections of the Right Platoon (Front line) will
        form a defensive flank in LEVANT TRENCH, and one section
        a defensive flank in LEVANT SUPPORT on the Southern
        boundary of the Raid.
        Remaining two Platoons (Front Line) will attack and
        mop-up LEVANT SUPPORT without halting in LEVANT TRENCH.
        Supporting Platoon will mop-up LEVANT TRENCH.

   (ii) 'C' (Left) Company will attack with 2 Platoons in Front
        and 2 Platoons in close support.

        Right Front Platoon - Objective. LEVANT SUPPORT from
        Q.10.b.95.75. to Northern Boundary.

        Right Support Platoon - Objective. LEVANT TRENCH from
        Q.10.b.85.65. to Northern Boundary including all works
        between this trench and the CRATER.

        Left Front Platoon - Objective. To enter Southern end
        of CRATER and proceed at once to Northern end to form
        a defensive flank.

                    (1)   /2 (c) (ii) Contd.

Contd - 2.

2. (c) (ii) Contd..

    Left Support Platoon will support the Left Front Platoon and mop up and examine the CRATER.

(d) **DIVIDING LINE BETWEEN COMPANIES.**

    Q.10.b.4.8. - Q.10.b.93.75. - Communication Trench Q.10.b.76.81 to Q.10.b.93.71. inclusive to 'D' (Right) Company.

(e) **USE OF LEWIS GUNS.**

    (i) The two Lewis Guns of the Right (Front) Platoon of 'D' Company will take up positions in LEVANT TRENCH to strengthen the Right Defensive Flank.

    (ii) The two Lewis Guns of the Left (Front) Platoon of 'C' Company will take up positions at the Northern end of the CRATER to strengthen the Left Defensive Flank.

    (iii) The remaining Platoons engaged will not carry Lewis Guns.

    (iv) During the Raid, all troops of the Left Company in our Front Line trenches will engage any hostile Machine Gun, that may open fire on our Raiding Party, from the North of NEW BEAUMONT ROAD with Lewis Gun and rifle fire.

3. (a) **HEADQUARTERS.**

    Headquarters of O.C., Raid and Advanced Battalion H.Q. will be at Q.10.b.3.3.

(b) **SPECIAL AMMUNITION.**

    It is requested that all 'P' bombs, Rockets, Lights, etc. required, be tested before being issued to the Raiding Party.

4. **PROPOSED ARTILLERY ARRANGEMENTS.**

(a) *Previous Preparation.*
    Artillery will be required to cut wire all along Battalion Front previous to night of raid.

(b) *Proposed Barrages, etc. (see tracing 'A'.)*

    (i) Zero to Zero plus 2 minutes - LEVANT TRENCH and CRATER.
    Zero plus 2 mins. to Zero plus 4 mins. - 1st Lift.
    Zero plus 4 mins. to Zero plus 6 mins. - 2nd Lift.
    Zero plus 6 mins. to Zero plus 30 mins - Forms box barrage.

    (ii) Two 4.5" Hows. will fire on LEVANT TRENCH where trench crosses grid line immediately North of CRATER, - from Zero to Zero plus 7 minutes.

    (iii) It is requested that the Valley North of the CRATER should receive especial artillery attention.

(c) *Outside Assistance.*
    It is requested that outside assistance be asked for as under :-

    (i) Portion of 38th. D.A. and 285rd R.F.A. Bde. to guard right Flank.

    (ii) Portion of 42nd. D.A. to guard Left Flank.

SECRET.
Contd - 2.

Para.4 (c)/(iii) Corps Heavy Artillery to block enemy approaches and shell known occupied areas.

(d) **Action of 6" Newton Trench Mortars**
The 3 6" Newton Trench Mortars are required for the following tasks :-

(a) 2 Mortars for the bombardment of 'Y' Ravine.
(b) 1 Mortar to thicken up barrage in Valley, North of the CRATER.

(e) **Action of 188th. L.T.M. Battery.**

The 188th. L.T.M. Battery is required to co-operate as under :-

Serial No.	No. of guns.	Situation.	Targets.	Remarks.
1.	3.	In bank - Q.4.c.6.7. to Q.4.c.8.d.	LEVANT TRENCH N. of CRATER.	Zero to zero plus 10 mins. rapid fire, then slow until 'close' signal goes up.
2.	4.	.... do ...	VALLEY N. of CRATER.	.... do ....
3.	1.	Q.10.d.8.7.	'Y' RAVINE.	To create a diversion. Zero minus 2 to Zero plus 4 minutes - rapid fire, then slow until 'close' signal goes up.

(f) **Duration of Barrages**
It is proposed that the Artillery Barrage should die down about Zero plus 35 minutes.

5. **MACHINE GUN BARRAGES.**

(a) **Action of 63rd. Machine Gun Battalion.**

The 63rd. M.G. Battalion will fire barrages as per tracing 'B' attached, - from Zero to Zero plus 60 minutes.

(b) **Outside assistance.**

It is requested that the 42nd. M.G. Battalion be asked to co-operate and guard the Left Flank.

Note on Artillery and Machine Gun Barrages.
It has been found by experience that directly our Artillery Barrage dies down, the enemy Artillery follows suit.
As it is anticipated that the raiders will return to their lines between Zero plus 35 and Zero plus 50 mins., it is proposed that the Artillery barrages cease at Zero plus 35 minutes (with guns ready to re-open if necessary) and it is hoped that, in consequence, the enemy's guns will follow suit, which will enable the raiders to return to their lines unmolested, after that hour. - The Machine Guns to keep up their fire up to Zero plus 60 minutes to cover retirement.

/Para 6.

Contd: - 4.

6. (a) PROPOSED ZERO HOUR.

There will be a small setting moon between 12 midnight (night 19th/20th) and 1-30 a.m., so any time between those hours will be convenient for Zero.

(b) SIGNALS.

(i) A telephone line will be laid to Raid Headquarters - Q.10.b.3.6.

(ii) If further bombardment is required, Artillery and Machine Guns will re-open on receiving code word "CARP"

(iii) Complete return of raiders will be notified by -

(a) Code word "PIKE" to all units concerned.
(b) A number of Rockets (colours to be detailed later).

(iv) To shew raiders direction of our lines, the following expedients will be resorted to :-

(a) White Very Lights will be frequently sent up from our Front Line from Zero plus 8 minutes onwards.
(b) Rattles will be frequently sounded.
(c) Bugle Calls will be sounded from time to time. (Battalion Call)

(c) MEDICAL.

(i) An Advanced Aid Post will be established at about Q.3.d.1.8

(ii) Relay Posts will be established in BEAUMONT RESERVE.

(iii) The 148th. Field Ambulance will be asked to supplement Battalion Stretcher Bearers.

(d) PRISONERS.

Prisoners will be sent to Q.10.b.3.6. where they will be carefully examined and handed over to escorts provided by troops not carrying out the raid for escort to Brigade Headquarters.

(e) COLLECTION of DOCUMENTS.

2 men will be detailed from each Platoon for the collection of documents etc. found in dugouts and on dead Germans. These men will carry sandbags for this purpose, and on return to our lines will deposit what they have collected at Q.10.b.3.6. (Advanced Battalion and Raid H.Q.)

(f) EQUIPMENT.

(i) All identifications will be removed from Raiders.
(ii) Men will carry rifles (bayonets fixed and dulled), 5 rounds in magazine - 1 Bandolier -, No other equipment.
(iii) Each Lewis Gun team (vide para. 2 (e) - (i) and (ii)) will take 9 magazines into action.
(iv) 2 men per section will carry 6 'P' bombs each in haversack, (vide para 3 (b))

/ Para 6 (f) (v).

(Contd - 5.)

Para 8. (f)/(v). 3 men per section will carry 6 Mills Bombs per
man in Haversack.
(vi) 2 pairs wire-cutters will be carried per Section.

Note re Recall Signal.

There will be no recall signal. - Platoons, when they have
accomplished their respective tasks, will be withdrawn under
orders of their own Commanders to our lines; Flank Guard
Platoons being the last to withdraw.

Runners
Bearings
H.Q.

J B Coleridge

Brigadier General,
Commanding -
88th. Inf. Brigade.

15/7/18.

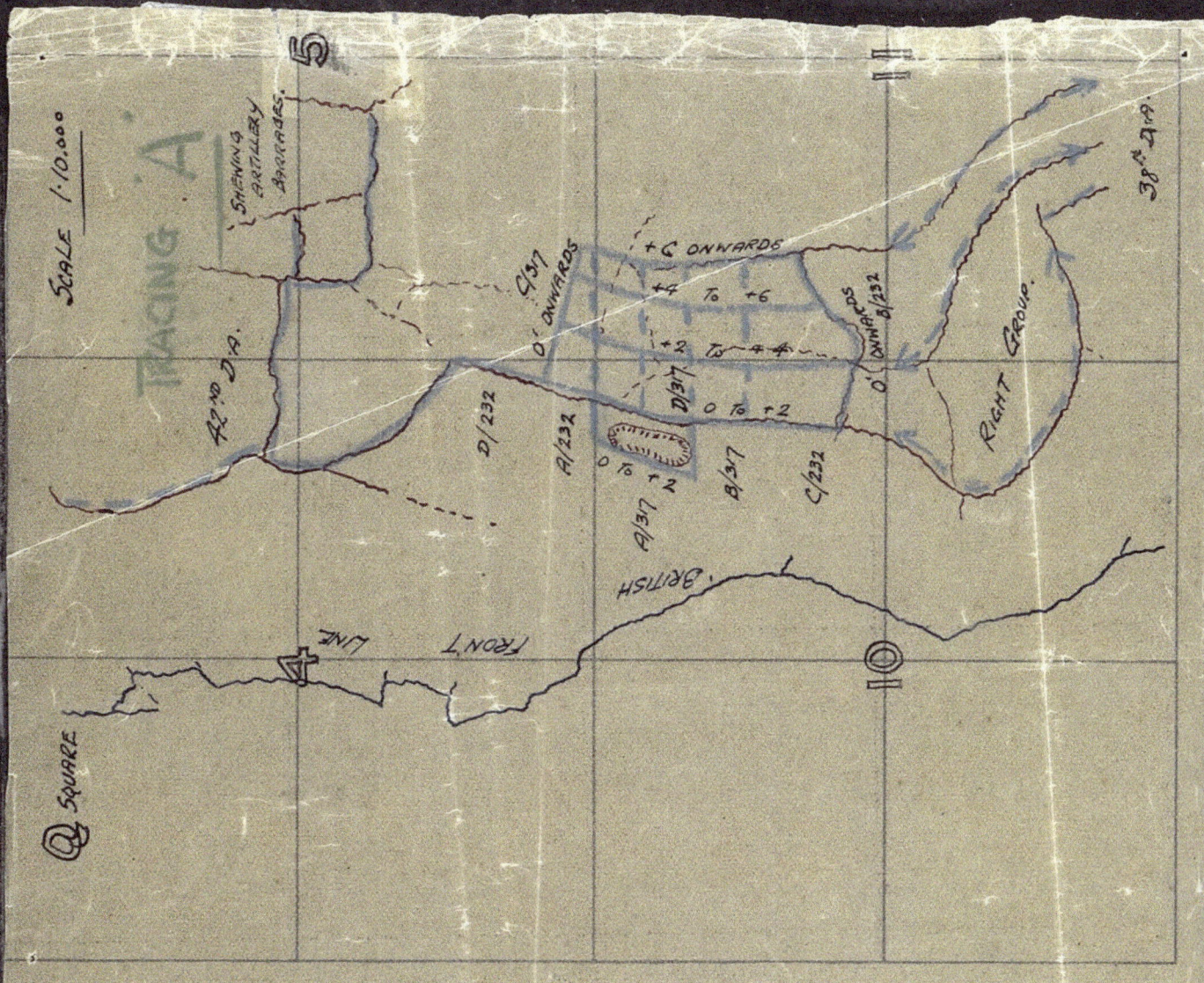

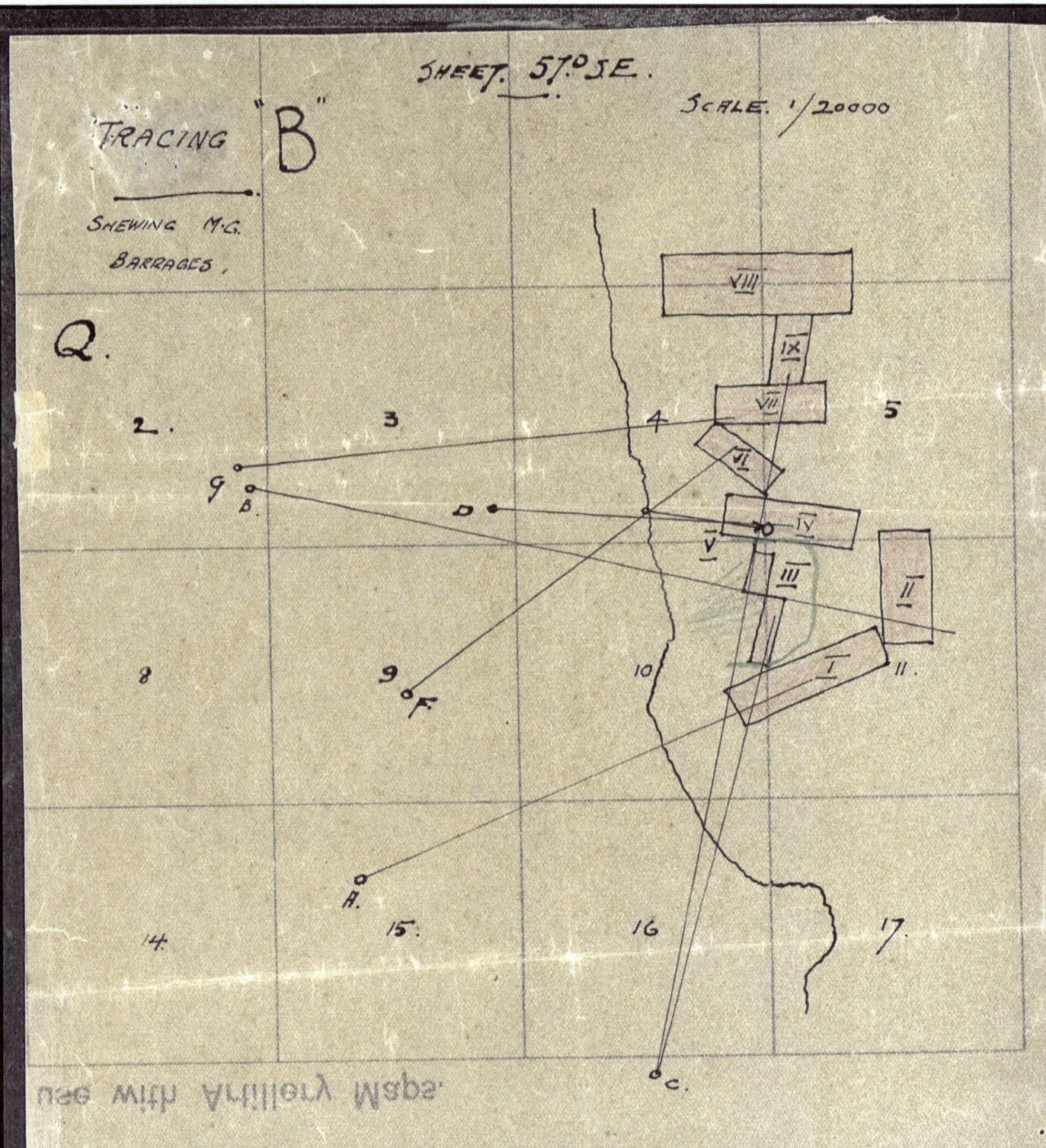

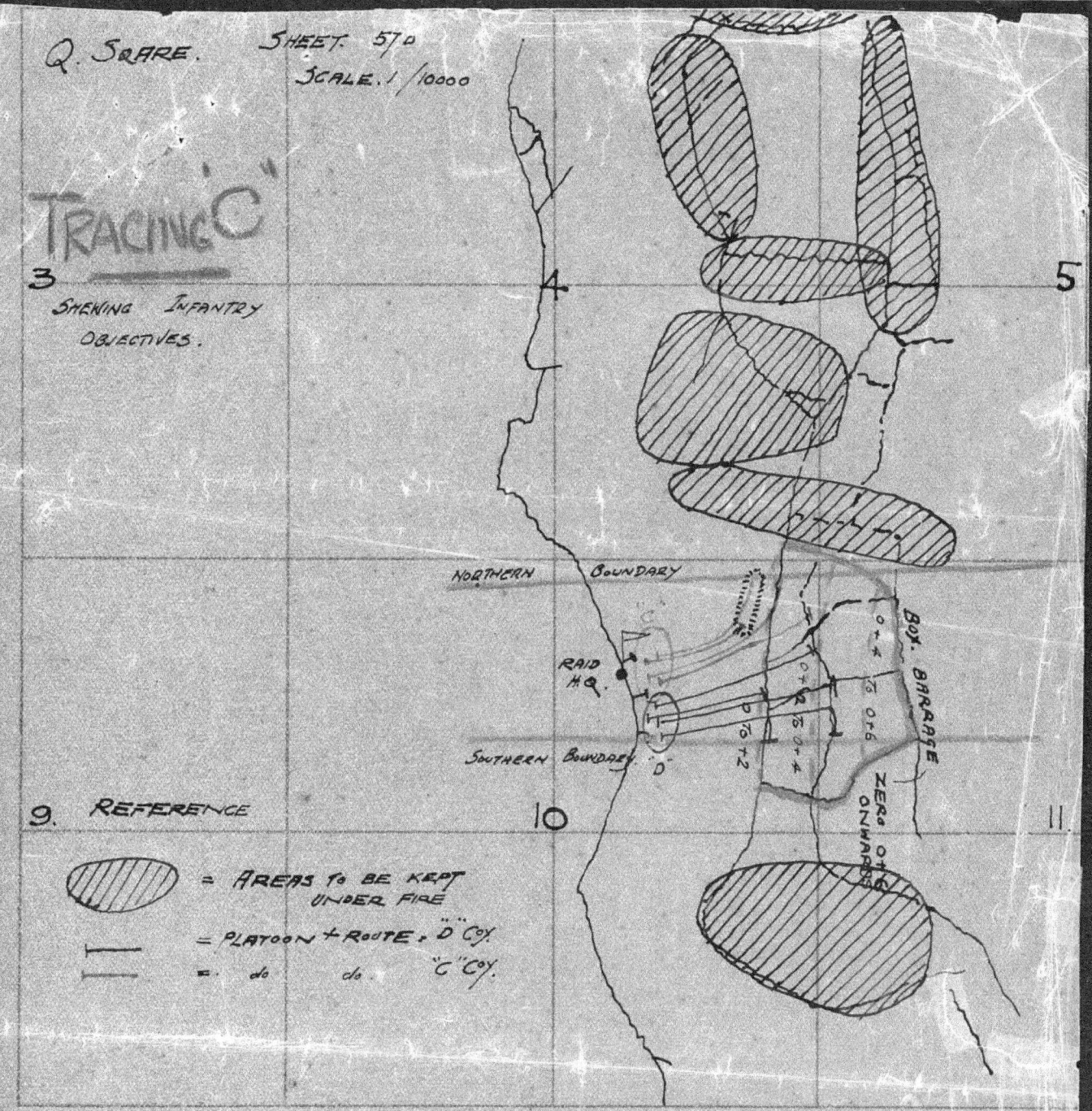

63rd. (RN) Division.   B.M. 1751.

A full report on the Raid carried out by the 2nd. Royal Irish Regiment on the night 19th/20th. July is forwarded herewith.
I have little to add to the remarks of the O.C., 2nd. Royal Irish Regiment in Sections III and IV attached with which I agree in general.

1. The Raid, although not as successful as had been hoped, appears to have been of value for the following reasons.

   (a) Considerable losses were inflicted on the enemy.
   (b) Identifications were procured.
   (c) Numbers of the enemy were seen running away, which must encourage not only the raiders, but all troops in the Brigade.

2. The employment of 2 Companies gave experience of what our Artillery fire, etc. is like to a considerable number of men of the Battalion, who had never been in an attack before.

3. It will be noticed that both Company Commanders employed led their men forward and were in the leading lines. In consequence one was wounded and the other lost for the time and all control vanished. While realizing their gallant conduct, I am of opinion that Commanders in a raid of this size should not be too far forward, at any rate to begin with, but should be located in some place in rear known to runners and others, where they should remain until the 1st. Objective is taken, after which they can move forward to the enemy's Front Line and re-organize for the next forward move.

4. The great value of previous rehearsals is brought out by this raid. I do not think it is too much to say that any success gained in this enterprise was largely due to these previous practices, which enabled, not only the Infantry, but also Artillery, Machine Gun and Trench Mortar Officers to form, beforehand, some appreciation of the problem in hand.

5. I do not agree with the O.C., 2nd. Royal Irish Regiment in his remarks regarding Rifle Bombs, and consider that had they been used to engage the Machine Guns encountered East of the CRATER, the Raid, very possibly, would have been completely successful.

6. The Artillery and Machine Gun arrangements appear to have been very good, and reflect, I consider, great credit on the Officers concerned in their preparation.

7. Appendices 'D' (63rd. (RN) Divisional Operation Order No. 208) and 'E' (63rd. (RN) M.G. Battn. Operation Order No. 44 with amendments) have not been attached, vide your reply to B.M. 1746 of 21/7/18 which states that these will be appended at Divisional Headquarters.

J D Coleridge

                                              Brigadier General,
                                                Commanding -
                                              188th. Infantry Brigade.
22/7/18.

188th. INFANTRY BRIGADE

REPORT ON RAID ON CRATER IN Q.10.b.
and ADJOINING TRENCHES.

by

2nd. Royal Irish Regt.

Night of July 19th/20th., 1918.

SECTION I.
GENERAL PREPARATIONS.

1. **SELECTION of OBJECTIVE :-**

    (i) It had been decided by the General Officer Commanding 188th. Infantry Brigade to carry out a Raid on the enemy's lines about the 18th./19th. July with the 2nd. Royal Irish Regt.

    Three portions of the line seemed to offer opportunities for a successful Raid. These were :-

    (a) The enemy's defences in Q.10.d. - West of 'Y' Ravine.

    (b) The enemy's defences between Q.11.a.10.80. and Q.4.b.90.00. including the CRATER.

    (c) The enemy's defences between Q.4.d.97.27. and Q.5.a.33.57.

    (ii) Owing to the following objections, (a) and (c) were rejected after careful consideration.

    (a) These defences had been successfully raided by the 190th. Inf. Brigade on the night of the 4th/5th. July, when identifications had been secured and casualties inflicted upon the enemy. There was, therefore, little reason for raiding this line again so soon. As the troops holding the area had been completely surprised on the occasion of the raid, it was thought that extreme alertness would now prevail. This, coupled with the other objections, was sufficient to make a raid on this section of line undesirable.

    (c) From Patrol Reports it appeared that few, if any, men were in occupation of the trenches in front (i.e. West) of this line. The advance which it was necessary to make from our Front Line, to ensure the capture of prisoners, was, therefore, nearly 700 yards, which was considered too great a depth for a small raid. This proposal was also, therefore, rejected.

    (b) - was finally decided upon, as there had been no raid upon that section of the line for some time. There was reason to believe that the enemy occupied the CRATER and adjoining trenches at night, and the presence of suspected dugouts, Machine Gun positions etc. pointed out that there was a possibility of inflicting material damage to his defences.

(1)

/ Para. 1(iii)

Contd. - 2.

Para. 1 contd.

    (iii) For the exact boundaries of the objectives chosen, see Appendix 'B' - BATTALION ORDER No. 17 - 2nd. Royal Irish Regt. and special map attached thereto.

2. PRELIMINARY CONFERENCES, ETC. :-

    (i) Permission having been received to carry out the raid, on the lines indicated, the Officer Commanding and other Officers and N.C.Os. of the 2nd. Royal Irish Regiment carried out preliminary reconnaissances of the ground on 10th. July.

    (ii) On July 14th. at 9-30 am. following the relief by the 2nd. Royal Irish Regt. of the 1st. Royal Marine Battalion in the line, a conference was held at Battalion Headquarters, at which the following were present :-

        188th. Infantry Brigade Commander.
        O.C., 232nd. Brigade R.F.A. (Left Group).
        O.C., 2nd. Royal Irish Regt.
        O.C., 63rd. (RN) Division Machine Gun Battalion.
        O.C., 188th. L.T.M. Battery.
        O.C., 'C' Company, 2nd. Royal Irish Regt.
        O.C., 'D' Company, 2nd. Royal Irish Regt.

    (iii) As a result of this conference, the Officer Commanding 2nd. Royal Irish Regt. forwarded his proposals on the night of the 14th. July, to 188th. Infantry Brigade Headquarters.

    (iv) Detailed plans based on these proposals were forwarded by the General Officer Commanding 188th. Infantry Brigade to Headquarters, 63rd. (RN) Division on 15th. July, and were approved.

    (v) The General Officer Commanding 188th. Infantry Brigade held frequent conferences, after these plans had been approved, with the Officers Commanding the 2nd. Royal Irish Regiment and the units which were to support the attack.

    (vi) For Orders issued by Commanders of Supporting Units see appendices of Section II. - PLAN.

3. PRELIMINARY ARTILLERY AND TRENCH MORTAR BOMBARDMENTS.

    (i) Wire-Cutting.
        The 232nd. Brigade R.F.A. commenced wire-cutting on 11th. July, 1918. Two 4.5" Howitzer Batteries (D/232 and D/317) were employed on this work with two 6" Newton Trench Mortars of Y/63rd. T.M. Battery.
        Wire was cut on the whole of the front to be raided, on the Eastern side of the CRATER and between LEVANT TRENCH and LEVANT SUPPORT.
        In order not to attract special attention to the objectives, wire was also cut at the same time at Q.10.d. and Q.4.b. and d.
        As the wire South and East of the CRATER could not be seen from our lines, registration on this wire was carried out with aeroplane observation.
        The localities in which wire was being cut were kept under intermittent 94.5" How., 18 pdr. and Lewis Gun fire during the night, to prevent repairs being carried out.

    (ii) Other Bombardments.
        Known and suspected Machine Gun emplacements from which fire could be directed upon the raiding area and assembly position were bombarded systematically by 4.5" Howitzer and Trench Mortars. Special attention was paid to the localities

Contd. - 3.

Para. 3 Contd.

(ii) - Contd.

Q.10.b.80.80., Q.4.d.90.00., Q.4.d.90.60. Q.11.a.05.50. and Q.10.b.90.15. and the CRATER.

(iii) For results of bombardments see Appendices 'G', 'H' and 'I' of Section III - EXECUTION.

4. PRELIMINARY PATROLLING.

The enemy's wire was patrolled nightly and reports on the progress of the wire cutting was rendered each day. Patrols also constantly reconnoitred the area to secure information regarding the enemy's defences and dispositions.

5. RELIEFS.

The Raiding Companies - 'C' and 'D' of the 2nd. Royal Irish Regt. were relieved by 'A' Company of the Anson Battalion in the line on the night of 16th. July, 1918. They carried out rehearsals and practices on the 17th. and 18th. and returned to the line again on the night of the 18th/19th. July. These reliefs gave an opportunity of instructing the men in the topography of the ground, in the general plan, and in the use of 'P' bombs.

6. INSTRUCTION OF RAIDERS.

(i) Rehearsals.

A taped course, on which were laid out in outline, our Front Line, the CRATER, LEVANT TRENCH and LEVANT SUPPORT, was prepared. The Raiders marched to this course on the morning of the 17th. July and the whole operation was practised.

The Officers Commanding the 232nd. Brigade R.F.A., Left Machine Gun Group -, 63rd. (RN) Division, and 188th L.T.M. Battery were present.

A second rehearsal was carried out on the 18th. July on similar lines and the men were instructed in the following :-

(a) Throwing of Bombs - 'P' and Mills No. 5.

(b) Light Signals - All the Light Signals which it was proposed to use in the attack were demonstrated several times.

(ii) Company Commanders frequently explained to each Platoon the part it had to play.

(iii) Special Maps and aerial photographs were also issued and explained to all Raiders

7. ASSEMBLY.

Gaps were cut in our wire just previous to the Assembly to facilitate the forming-up of our troops beyond. Tapes were laid to give the general direction of their advance to the Raiders. The Assembly Positions were also taped out.

J D Coleridge

21/7/18.

Brigadier General,
Commanding -
188th. Inf. Brigade.

REPORT ON RAID ON CRATER in Q.10.b.

and ADJOINING TRENCHES.

by

2nd. Royal Irish Regiment - night 19/20th. July, 1918.

Reference Sheet 57.D. SE, - 1/20,000.

INDEX.

SECTION I.

GENERAL PREPARATIONS FOR RAID.

SECTION II.

PLAN.

SECTION III.

EXECUTION

SECTION IV.

NOTES and LESSONS.

APPENDICES.

SECTION II - PLAN.

- (A) - 188th. Infantry Brigade Order No. 204.
- B. - 2nd. Royal Irish Regt. Order No. 17.
- C. - (i) - 'C' Company - 2nd. R. Ir. Regt. - SPECIAL ORDERS.
   (ii) - 'D' Company - 2nd. R. Ir. Regt. - SPECIAL ORDERS.
- D. - 63rd. (RN) Divisional Operation Order No. 208.
- E. - 63rd. (RN) Machine Gun. Battn. Operation Order No. 44.) with Amendments)
- F. - 188th. L.T.M. Battery - Order No. 14.

SECTION III. - EXECUTION.

MAP ONE.

- G. - Report on Operations by O.C., 232nd. Brigade R.F.A.
- H. - " " " " " " Left Group - 63rd. (RN) Machine Gun Battalion.
- I. - " " " " " " O.C., 188th. L.T.M. Battery.

SECTION II.

PLAN.

For details of PLAN see following Appendices :-

A. - 188th. Infantry Brigade Order No. 204.

B. - 2nd. Royal Irish Regt. Order No. 17.

C. - (i) 'C' Company Order.
     (ii) 'D' Company Order.

D. - 63rd. (RN) Divisional ARTILLERY Operation Order No. 208.

E. - 63rd. (RN) Machine Gun Battalion Operation Order No. 44.

F. - 188th. L.T.M. Battery Order No. 14.

T. S. Coleridge

Brigadier General,
Commanding -
188th. Inf. Brigade.

22/7/18.

Appendices B. D. and E forwarded to 63(RN) Division only.

APPENDIX A
SECTION II PLAN
SECRET.
Copy No...........

188th. INF. BRIGADE ORDER No. 204.

Reference - Sheet 57.D. SE. - 1/20,000.

1. The 2nd. Royal Irish Regt. will carry out a raid on the enemy's trenches at an hour and on a date to be notified later, with the object of :-

    (a). Inflicting loss on the enemy.
    (b). Securing identifications.
    (c). Destroying any dugouts met with and capturing and destroying Machine Guns and Trench Mortars found in the area.
    (d). Examining CRATER and ascertaining if enemy has commenced mining therefrom.

2. OBJECTIVES :-

    1st. Objective :- LEVANT TRENCH between Q.10.b.80.40 and Q.10.b.87.95., including CRATER.

    2nd. Objective :- LEVANT SUPPORT between Q.11.a. 10.40. and Q.11.a. 00.90. Patrols to be sent out as far as protective barrage admits.

3. STRENGTH of RAIDING PARTY.

    1 Officer - (O.C., Raid).
    4 other Officers, and 2 Companies (150 O.Rs.)

4. ZERO HOUR and DATE OF RAID.

    Zero Hour and Date of Raid will be notified later to all concerned.

5. ASSEMBLY :-

    The Raiding Companies will form up in front of our wire between Q.10.B.5.3. and Q.10.b.4.8., being in position at Zero minus 15 minutes.

6. WITHDRAWAL :-

    There will be no recall signal. Platoons, when they have accomplished their respective tasks, will be withdrawn under orders of their own Commanders to our lines; Flank Guard Platoons being the last to withdraw.

7. DANGER POINTS :-

    The following stretches of trench in our Front Line must be avoided by raiders returning to our lines, as the fire of hostile Machine Guns will render these dangerous -

    (i) Q.10.d.2.5. to Q.10.b.2.2.
    (ii) Q.10.b.2.8. to Q.4.d.0.3.

8. ARTILLERY, TRENCH MORTAR, and MACHINE GUN SUPPORT.

    Details of these will be issued separately as Appendices, to those concerned.

/Para. 9.

Contd.- 2.

9. SIGNALS :-

   (i) The following Light Signals will be used -

   (a) A Rifle Grenade (Colour to be notified later) will be fired three times in succession from our Front Line trench, opposite the point raided, under orders to be issued by the O.C., Raid, as soon as all the raiding party have returned. On this signal the Artillery and Machine Gun Barrage will die down.

   (b) In addition, Light Signals (colour to be notified later) will be fired during the time the raid is in progress, from our Front Line, to indicate its position to the raiders.

   (ii) In addition to these Signals the following Code Words will be used :-

   (a) "PIKE" - to indicate the return of the Raiders.

   (b) "CARP" - to secure further Artillery and Machine Gun bombardment, if necessary, after the barrage has ceased.

   (iii) The Battalion Call will be sounded on the Bugle, and Rattles will be frequently sounded. These will be used to supplement the lights used to indicate the position of our line.

10. The Brigade Signal Officer will arrange to connect up the Headquarters of the O.C., Raid with the Advanced Forward Zone Battalion Headquarters by fullerphone.

11. SYNCHRONIZATION of WATCHES.:-

   Watches will be synchronized as follows :-

   (a) An Officer from each of the following will report at Brigade Headquarters for this purpose at 5-45 pm. on the day of the raid :-

   232nd. Bde. R.F.A. (Left Group)
   Left Group - 63rd. Machine Gun Battalion.

   (b) An Officer from 188th. Inf. Bde. H.Q. will report at the Headquarters of the 2nd. R. Ir. Regt. for the purpose of synchronizing watches with Officer representatives of the following units, at 7-00 pm. on the day of the raid :-

   2nd. Royal Irish Regt.
   188th. L.T.M. Battery.

12. ADMINISTRATIVE ARRANGEMENTS.

   Arrangements for escorting Prisoners, Medical Arrangements, etc., will be issued later as an appendix.

/ Para. 13.

Contd - 3.

13. O.C., 2nd. Royal Irish Regt. will forward to 188th. Inf. Bde. Headquarters, three copies of his detailed orders for the Raid, not later than 6 p.m., 18th. July, 1918.

14. ACKNOWLEDGE.

H. Steele
Captain,
A/Brigade Major,
188th. Inf. Brigade.

17/7/18.

Issued to Sigs. at ..11..p.m....

Copies to :-

1. File.
2. War Diary.
3. Staff Captain.
4. R.M. Battalion.
5. Anson Battalion.
6. 2/R. Irish Regt.
7. O.C., Raid.
8. No. 2 Sig. Section.
9. Left M.G. Group.
10. 188th. Inf. Bde. Transport Offr.
11. " L.T.M.Bty.
12. 63rd. (RN) Div. 'G'.
13. " " " 'Q'.
14. 189th. Inf. Bde.
15. 125th. Inf. Bde.
16. 190th. Inf. Bde.
17. 249th. Fd. Coy. R.E.
18. 63rd. (RN) Div. M.G. Bn.
19. 148th. Fd. Ambulance
20. 252nd. Bde. R.F.A.

APPENDIX lV. to 188th Infantry Brigade Order No. 204.

ADMINISTRATIVE ARRANGEMENTS.

RAID IDENTITY DISCS.

Every Officer and man of the Raiding Party will be issued with duplicate red Identity Discs stamped with the Index Letter N.K. and a serial number. One of these Special Raid Identity Discs will be worn by each Officer and man in the place of the ordinary Identity Discs, which will be retained by the Battalion, the corresponding duplicate Raid Identity Disc being securely fastened thereto.

On return from the raid, the Raid Identity Disc which has been worn in the raid, will be handed back by the Officer and man in exchange for the two ordinary Identity Discs, care being taken that the corresponding raid disc is detached therefrom.

On completion of the raid the special Raid Identity Discs will be returned to Brigade Headquarters.

PRISONERS.

A special party under the supervision of an officer will be detailed for collecting prisoners and escorting them to Brigade Headquarters. It is of the utmost importance that prisoners should be sent on to Brigade Headquarters as rapidly as possible, and therefore the escorting party must be well acquainted with the best route back. All wounded prisoners, except those, who in the opinion of the M.O. are not fit to do so, will be included amongst those sent to Brigade Headquarters.

Receipts will be given for all prisoners handed over or taken over by the escorts.

The attention of all men employed on Escort duty will be drawn to G.R.Os 3823 and 3987.

MEDICAL.

An Advanced Aid Post will be established at about Q.3.d.1.3.

Relay Posts will be established in BEAUMONT

RESERVE.

The 148th Field Ambulance will be asked to supplement Battalion Stretcher Bearers. M.O. 2nd Royal Irish Regiment will arrange all details with O.C. 148th Field Ambulance.

To all recipients of 188th Inf. Brigade Order No. 204.

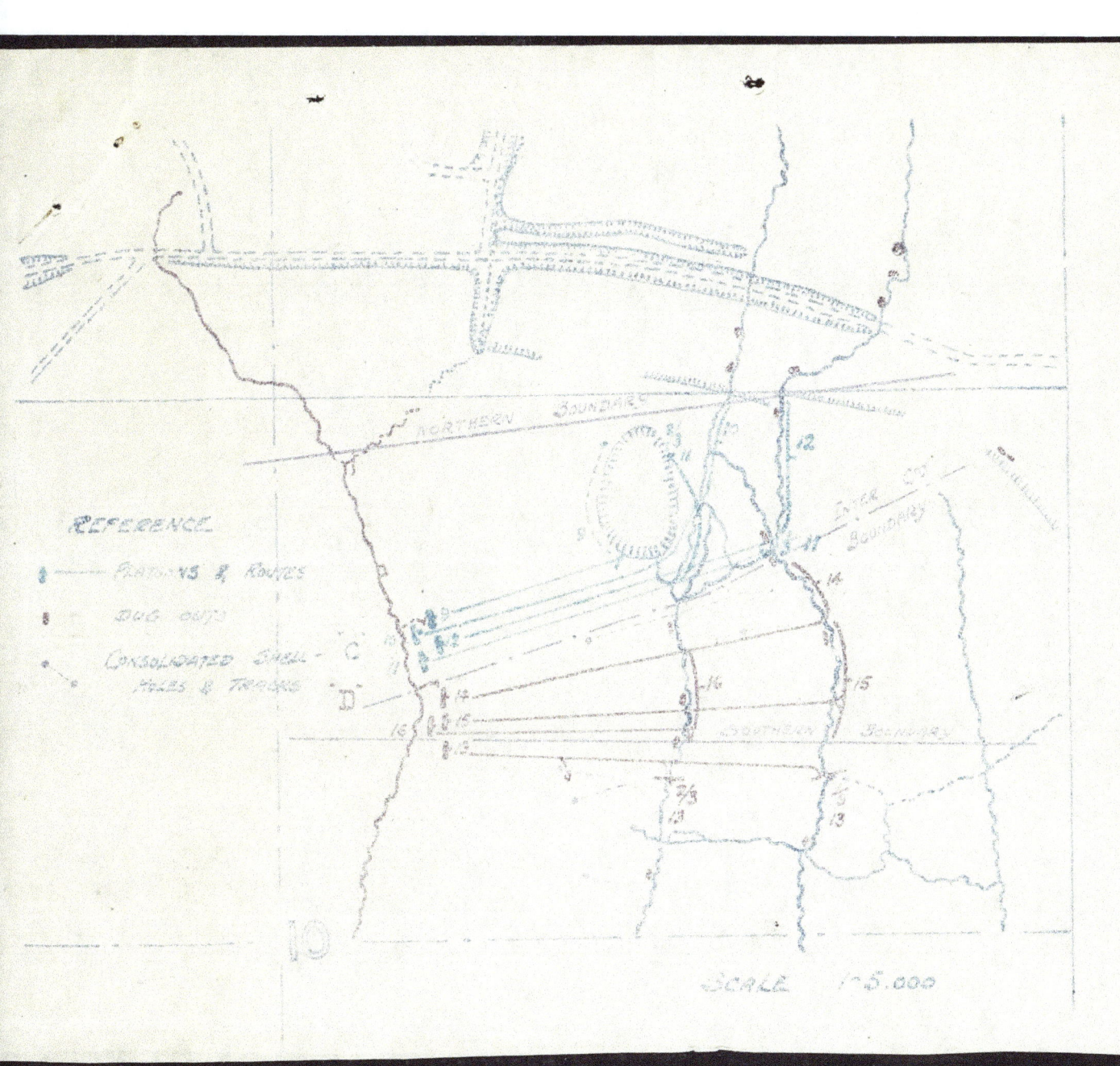

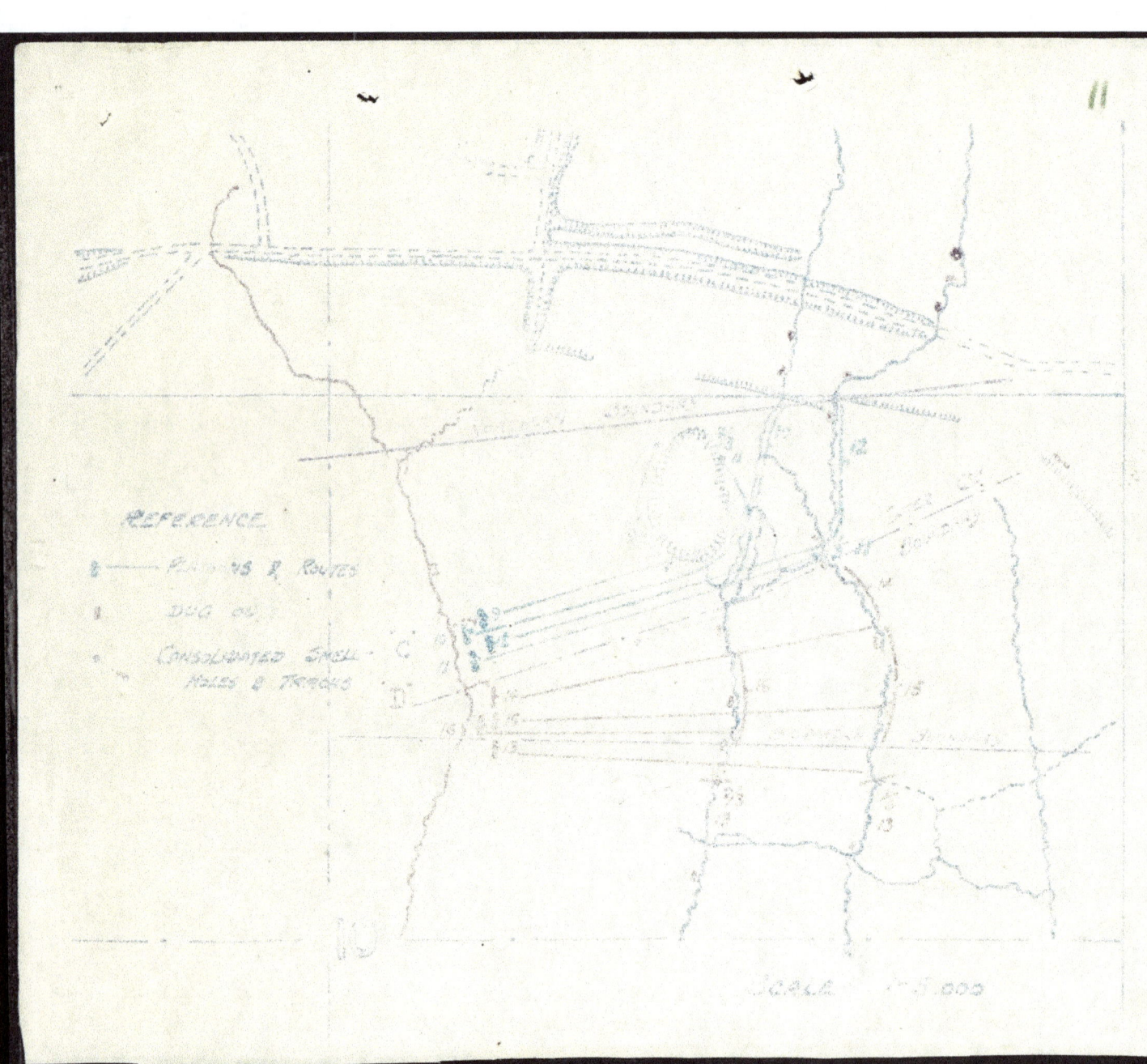

SECRET.
Copy No. 18

2nd. Battalion - The ROYAL IRISH REGIMENT - Order No. 17.

Ref./ Special Map attached
and 57.D. SE. - 1/20,000.

---

1. INTENTION.

    On a date and at a time to be notified later, the Battalion will carry out a raid on the CRATER and enemy trenches in the vicinity to the East and South, with the object of -

    (a) Inflicting loss on the enemy.

    (b) Securing identifications.

    (c) Destroying any dugouts met with and capturing or destroying any Machine Guns and Trench Mortars found in the area.

    (d) Examining CRATER and ascertaining if enemy has commenced mining therefrom.

2. INFORMATION.

    The enemy is believed to be holding CRATER, LEVANT TRENCH and LEVANT SUPPORT. By night Machine Guns are sometimes placed in fortified shell holes in front of LEVANT TRENCH. The Eastern edge of CRATER is believed to be held. From aeroplane photographs, dugouts have been located as shewn on attached map.

3. OBJECTIVES.

    1st. Objective.
    To occupy S.W. edge of CRATER, combined with a frontal attack on LEVANT TRENCH between CRATER and Q.10.b.77.35.

    2nd. Objective.
    To penetrate enemy's position as far as LEVANT SUPPORT between Q.11.a.04.35, and Q.10.b.97.98.

    3rd. Objective.
    To attack CRATER from East and South.

4. BOUNDARIES.

    Right - Q.10.b.77.35. to Q.11.a.04.35.
    Left - Q.10.b.69.95. to Q.10.b.97.98.
    Inter-Company - Q.10.b.76.61. to Q.10.b.95.71.

5. TROOPS TO BE USED.

    'C' and 'D' Companies (strength 5 Officers and 150 O.Rs.) will carry out the raid, directly supported by -

    232nd. and 317th. R.F.A. Brigades.
    64 Guns of 63rd. (RN) Division Machine Gun Battalion.
    168th. L.T.M.Battery.
    Three 6" Newton Mortars.

    In addition, the 223rd. R.F.A. Brigade, portions of 42nd. Div. Artillery - 38th. Div. Artillery, and 42nd. Machine Gun Battalion will guard the flanks of the raid.

(1) /Para. 6.

Contd. - 2.

6. **FORMING UP PLACE.**

   'D' Company (Right)   Q.10.b.32.32. to Q.10.b.31.47.
   'C' Company (Left)   Q.10.b.31.47. to Q.10.b.28.61.

7. **PLAN of ATTACK.**

   (a) 'D' (Right) Company will attack with 3 platoons in Front and one in close support.
   Two Sections of the Right Front Platoon will form a defensive flank in LEVANT TRENCH, attacking any Machine Gun that may open fire from shell holes on the Southern Boundary ; and one Section a defensive flank in LEVANT SUPPORT on the Southern boundary of the raid.
   Remaining two platoons (Front Line) will attack and mop up LEVANT SUPPORT without halting in LEVANT TRENCH.
   Supporting Platoon will mop up LEVANT TRENCH.

   (b) 'C' (Left) Company will attack with two Platoons in Front and two Platoons in close support.
   <u>Right Front Platoon</u> passing South of CRATER, without halting in LEVANT TRENCH, will attack LEVANT SUPPORT between the Company boundaries.
   <u>Left Front Platoon</u> to form a defensive flank, two Sections to occupy Southern edge of CRATER and subsequently attack and mop up CRATER in conjunction with an attack from East by Right Support Platoon, and one Lewis Gun Section to work round Western edge of CRATER.

   <u>Left Support Platoon</u>, passing South of CRATER, to attack LEVANT TRENCH between Company boundaries.

   <u>Right Support Platoon</u> - One Section to mop up LEVANT SUPPORT and all ground between this trench and LEVANT TRENCH, Remaining two Sections passing South of CRATER, along LEVANT TRENCH, will attack CRATER from East in conjunction with attack from South by Left Front Platoon.

8. **EQUIPMENT.**

   (i) All identifications will be removed from raiders.

   (ii) Men will carry Rifles, (Bayonets fixed and dulled), 5 rounds in magazine and 1 bandolier. No other equipment.

   (iii) The Lewis Gun Sections of Platoons forming defensive flanks will each carry two Lewis Guns with 9 magazines per gun. No other Lewis Guns will be brought on raid.

   (iv) Two men per Section will carry 6 'P' Bombs No 27, each, in haversack.

   (v) Three men per Section will carry 6 Mills Bombs each in haversack.

   (vi) 2 Pairs Wire Cutters will be carried per Section. All Platoon Commanders and understudies will also carry wire cutters.

   (vii) Box Respirators will be carried by all ranks.

/ Para. 9.

Contd. - 3.

9. ARTILLERY ARRANGEMENTS.

 (a) Barrages :- Zero to Zero plus 4 mins. - LEVANT TRENCH & CRATER.
      Zero plus 4 to Zero plus 6 mins.- 1st. Lift. -
                  (100 yards)
      Zero plus 6 to Zero plus 8 mins.- 2nd. Lift. -
                  (100 yards)
      Zero plus 8 to Zero plus 60 mins. - Forms Box
                    Barrage.

 (b) Two 4.5" Hows. will fire on LEVANT TRENCH at Q.4.d.86.00. from Zero to Zero plus 7 minutes.

 (c) 223rd. R.F.A. Brigade and portion of 38th. Division Artillery will guard Right Flank.

 (d) Portion of 42nd. Division Artillery will guard Left Flank.

 (e) Corps Heavy Artillery will block enemy approaches and shell known occupied areas.

 (f) Two 6" Newton Mortars will bombard 'Y' RAVINE and One will thicken up barrage in Valley, North of CRATER.

10. L.T.M. BATTERY.

 (a) 3 guns on LEVANT TRENCH at Q.4.d.86.00.
 (b) 4 guns in Valley, North of CRATER.
 (c) 1 gun in 'Y' Ravine at Q.10.d.6.7.

11. MACHINE GUNS.

 (a) Form a Box Barrage.
 (b) Thicken barrage on Left Flank.

All Machine Guns will open fire as soon as it is obvious that Artillery barrage has started, but not later than Zero plus 1.

12. COMMUNICATIONS.

 (i) Telephone at Raid Headquarters.

 (ii) If further bombardment is required, Artillery and Machine Guns will re-open on receiving Code Word "CARP".

 (iii) Complete return of raiders will be notified by :-

  (a) Code word "PIKE" to all units concerned.
  (b) A Light Signal, colour of which will be notified later.

 (iv) (a) To guide raiders out, tracer ammunition will be fired along flanks.

  (b) There will be no signal to withdraw. Platoon Commanders will order their Platoons to retire when task allotted has been completed, notifying units on Right and Left that they are doing so. Units forming defensive flanks retire with adjacent platoons.

  (c) To show raiders direction of our lines, red and white lights will be sent up from our Front Line from Zero plus 20 minutes.

  (d) Runners are to be used during raid to communicate with Flanks and Raid Headquarters. 2 runners will be sent to Raid H.Q. at Zero plus 40.

/Para. 13.

Contd. - 4.

13. **MEDICAL ARRANGEMENTS.**

    (a) An Advanced Aid Post will be established in Front Line at Q.5.b.2.1.

    (b) Relay Posts will be established in BEAUMONT RESERVE.

    (c) 148th. Field Ambulance will supplement Battalion Stretcher Bearers.

14. **PRISONERS.**

    Prisoners will be sent to 'B' Company Headquarters in BEAUMONT RESERVE (Q.10.c.2.7.), where they will be examined and despatched to Brigade H.Q. under arrangements to be made by O.C., 'B' Company.

15. **COLLECTION of DOCUMENTS.**

    2 men will be detailed from each Platoon for the collection of documents etc. found in dugouts and on dead Germans. These men will carry haversacks for this purpose, and on return will hand over what they have found to O.C., 'B' Coy. at Q.10.c.2.7. ('B' Company's H.Q.)

16. Raid Headquarters and Advanced Battalion Headquarters will be established at Q.10.b.35.50.

17. ACKNOWLEDGE.

M. E. C. Harrison
Lieut.- Colonel,
Cmdg. - 2nd. Royal Irish Regt.

18/7/18.

Issued at 8.30 a.m.

Distribution :-

Copy No. 1. 188th. Inf. Bde.
"   "   2. "   "   "
"   "   3. 'A' Coy. - 2nd. R. Ir. Regt.
"   "   4. 'B' "   "   "   "   "
"   "   5. 'C' "   "   "   "   "
"   "   6. 'D' "   "   "   "   "
"   "   7. 188th. L.T.M.Bty.
"   "   8.)
"   "   9.)
"   " 10.) Left Group Artillery.
"   " 11.)
"   " 12. 63rd. Div. M.G. Bn.
"   " 13.   "   "   "   "
"   " 14. Anson Battalion.
"   " 15. R.M. Battalion.
"   " 16. Adjoining Bn. - 189th. Inf. Bde.
"   " 17.   "   " - 125th. Inf. Bde.
"   " 18. Diary.
"   " 19.   "
"   " 20. File.

SECRET.
Copy No... 18 ....

AMENDMENT No. 1.
to
2nd. Royal Irish Regiment -- Order No. 17.

Ref. - 57.d. S.E. - 1/20,000
and Special map issued with Order No.17.

1. To para. 1 - INTENTION , add :-

   The Raid will be carried out on night, 19th./20th.July.

   Zero hour 12-15 am.

2. Para. 9 ARTILLERY ARRANGEMENTS, delete sub-section (a) and substitute :-

   "(a) BARRAGES - Zero to Zero plus 4 minutes -
   LEVANT TRENCH and CRATER (This barrage will lift off CRATER at Zero plus 2.)

   Zero plus 4 to Zero plus 7 - 1st. Lift.
   (100 yards)
   Zero plus 7 to Zero plus 9.- 2nd. Lift.
   (100 yards)
   Zero plus 9 to Zero plus 60. Form box barrage.

3. Para. 12 COMMUNICATIONS.(i) to sub-para. (iii) (b) add :-

   "The Light Signal will be a series of white asteroid floating Lights".

   (ii) delete sub-para (iv) (b) and substitute :-

   "(iv) (b) 'D' Company, on completion of task allotted will fire a series of Green Very Lights in an Easterly direction.
   'C' Company, on completion of task allotted will fire a series of Red Very Lights in an Easterly direction.

   There will be no withdrawal until both red and green Very Lights have been fired, when the two Companies will retire simultaneously under Company Commanders' orders.

   (iii) To Sub-para (c) add :-

   " A bugler will sound the Regimental Call at frequent intervals in the Front Line Trench , commencing at Zero plus 20.
   Lowis Guns in Front Line Trench will fire bursts of tracer ammunition in to the air on either flank of forming up positions.

4. Add para. 18 DANGER POINTS
   The following stretches of trench in our Front Line must be avoided by raiders returning to our lines as the fire of hostile Machine Guns will render these dangerous :-

   (i) Q.10.d.2.5. to Q.10.b.2.2.
   (ii) Q.10.b.2.8. to Q.4.d.0.3.

Contd. - 2.

5. Add para. 19. SYNCHRONIZATION of WATCHES.

    Watches will be synchronized at Battalion Headquarters at 7-30 pm.

    Company Commanders will arrange to have at least 3 watches per Company at that hour, at Bn.H. Remaining watches to be synchronized under Company arrangements.

6. ACKNOWLEDGE.

                                    M. C. C. Harrison
                                    Lieut. - Colonel,
                                    Commanding
18/7/18.   2nd. Bn. Royal Irish Regt.

Issued to all recipients of 2nd. Bn. R. Irish Regt. Order No. 17.

L. Sanderson

MOONLIGHT CHART for July, August & September, 1918

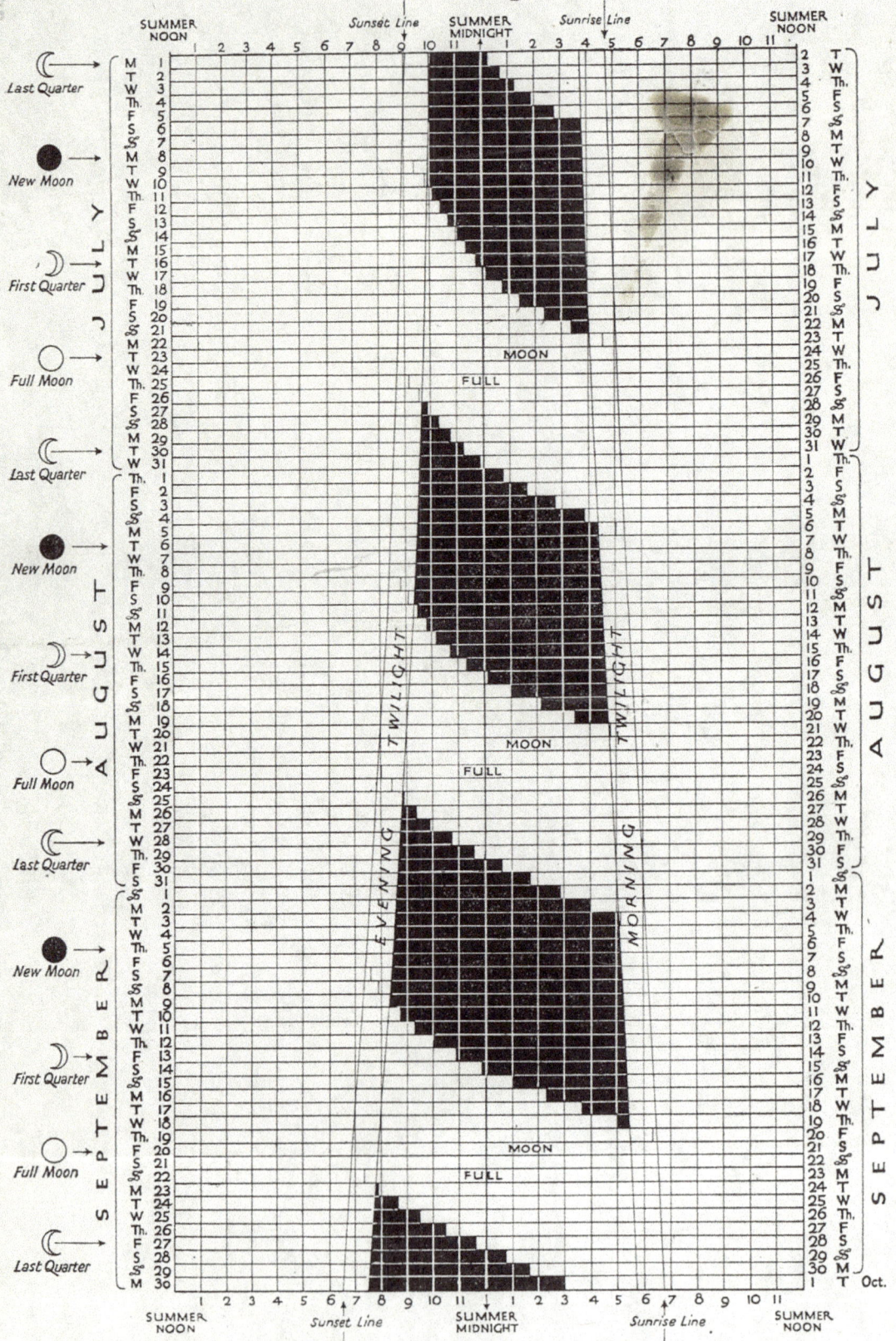

Times of sunrise are taken from Field Almanac, and computed for a point in the neighbourhood of Bethune

SECRET.

2nd. Battalion THE ROYAL IRISH REGT.

Copy. No.....

Ref. Map - 57.d. S.E. and special map
issued to Battn. Cmdrs.

APPENDIX (I)

'C' COMPANY.
SPECIAL ORDERS.

SECTION II PLAN

1. Issued to 'C' Company to supplement Battalion Order No. 17 dated 18/7/18 which has been read out and fully explained to all ranks concerned ; the Company, collectively and by Sections, having been brought several times over a facsimile taped course shewing all objectives. Special Maps and Photographs have been issued to all Platoon Commanders.

2. DRESS and EQUIPMENT.

   (a) STEEL HELMETS (JACKETS will NOT be worn), sleeves well rolled up, BOX RESPIRATORS at the 'ALERT' position, RIFLES, 5 rounds in magazine and 1 Bandolier. BAYONETS will be dulled and shall be fixed in NO MAN'S LAND on a signal from Platoon Commander. ALL BOMBERS will wear HAVERSACKS for carrying BOMBS. The two Lewis Guns will have 9 magazines EACH. ALL Platoon Commanders and understudies and 2 men in every Section will carry WIRE CUTTERS.

   (b) Platoon Commanders will make arrangements to inspect, carefully, men's equipment etc., and personally inspect all bombs, taking care that the pins in Mills Bombs have been prepared for easy drawing.

3. ASSEMBLY.

   Platoons will be ready to move off from their respective POSTS at 9-30 p.m. and will be led by the special guides via BOWERY AVENUE to the Front Line at the points where the wire has been cut to facilitate quick assembly in NO MAN'S LAND. On a signal from O.C., Company, Platoons will be led on to the tape in front, forming up in two lines as follows :-

   No. 9 - LEFT FRONT.   No. 12 - RIGHT FRONT.
   No. 10- LEFT SUPPORT.   No. 11. - RIGHT SUPPORT.

4. ACTION of PLATOONS.

   When the Artillery Barrage commences, on a Signal from O.C., Company, all ranks will crawl forward to within a safe distance from bursting shells. When the barrage lifts, ALL will rush forward to first Objectives, Nos. 10 and 12 Platoons passing over the first Objectives and preparing for the charge to final objective , in the meantime No. 11 and two Sections of No. 9 with a Section of Lewis Guns will enter the CRATER from West and East simultaneously.

5. WITHDRAWAL.

   (a) The Signal to withdraw will be fired from the line of the final objective. A succession of RED Very Lights fired in direction of Enemy will be 'C' Company's Signal. GREEN Very Lights will be 'D' Company's Signal. The withdrawal will not commence until after BOTH those signals have been fired. All ranks to thoroughly understand this.

/ 5 (b)

Contd. - 2.

5. WITHDRAWAL - Contd.

    (b)   Rockets consisting of two RED and two WHITE Lights will be fired continuously from our Lines to guide all ranks back. The Bugle will sound the Regimental Call also.

    (c)   Nos. 10 and 12 Platoons will withdraw through Nos. 9 & 11. Care must be taken to return over the ground by which the advance was made and all casualties that may be found will be brought back to our Lines.

    (d)   All men returning to our Front Line will turn to the Left and pass along, proceeding (after reporting to their Platoon Commander, or understudy detailed, that they are back) along BUFFS AVENUE, and thence by Road or BOVRIL TRENCH to their respective localities in SUPPORT LINE.

    (e)   All Runners will be directed to Battalion and Company FORWARD H.Q. in FRONT LINE.

    (f)   STRETCHER BEARERS will be directed to the FORWARD AID POST.

    (g)   All men on returning to SUPPORT LINES will report at Company H.Q. to Company Clerk - L/Cpl. JAMES.

6. DOCUMENTS etc.

    (a)   All bodies which may be found will be stripped of identifications and documents which will be carefully brought back in SANDBAGS to O.C., 'B' Company by those specially detailed.

    (b)   All dugouts will be thoroughly searched for identifications and documents.

                                    (sgd.) J. PIKE.
                                                Captain,
                                                O.C. 'C' Coy.

Issued at Conference of Officers
and N.C.Os. at 9-30 a.m., 19/7/18.

Copy. No. 1. - O.C., 'D' Company (Right Flank)
   "   " 2. - Col. Harrison, M.C. - Cmdg. Battalion.
   "   " 3. -
   "   " 4. - File.

APPENDIX (#) SECTION II
PLAN

SECRET.

SPECIAL ORDER issued to 'D' Company to supplement Battalion Order No. 17, which has been read out and fully explained to all ranks.

Ref. Map 57.d.SE. 1/20,000
and Special Map issued to all Platoon Cmdrs.

1. **ZERO HOUR.**
   Zero hour 12-15 a.m. - night of 19th./20th. July.

2. **ASSEMBLY.**

   (a) No. 13 and 14 Platoons will commence to close in at 10-30 p.m.
   No. 15 and 16 Platoons will be ready to move off from SUPPORT at 10-45 p.m. and will form up -
   No. 15 on RIGHT, No. 16 - LEFT.
   No. 13 Platoon will move off under guide to position already chosen at 11-00 p.m.
   No. 14 Platoon will move off under guide at 10-55 pm.
   No. 15 Platoon will move off under guide at 10-46 pm.
   No. 16 Platoon will move off under guide at 10-47 pm.

   (b) When marching into position, all ranks are again reminded of yesterdays conference.

   (c) At 11-30 pm. No. 13 Platoon will move into position in NO MAN'S LAND under guides already detailed.
   No. 14, 15, 16 Platoons to follow, No. 15 following No. 13.
   No. 14 following No. 15.
   No. 16 following No. 14.

   (d) Disposition of Company will be :-

   No. 13 - Left. - on Right Flank of 'C' Coy.
   No. 15. Centre.
   No. 14 - Right Flank.
   No. 16 - in rear of No. 15.

3. **DRESS.**

   (a) Rifles with Bayonets fixed, dulled.
   (b) Box Respirators will be worn by all ranks.
   (c) Haversacks will be worn by men already detailed to carry 'P' bombs, No. 5.
   (d) All identifications will be removed. Special identification discs will be issued later.
   (e) Platoon Cmds. will inspect men's equipment and bombs.

4. **SIGNAL for ADVANCE.**

   Platoon Commanders will note barrage, and must be careful that they do not get too close. All ranks are reminded of yesterdays conference.

5. **PLAN of ATTACK.**

   No. 13 Platoon on LEFT. One Section on Left must keep in touch with 'C' Coy. At final Objective two Sections will mop up.

   No. 14 Platoon. At 1st. Objective one Section and Lewis Gun Section will form a defensive flank in LEVANT TRENCH.
   At final Objective No. 14 Platoon will form defensive flank in LEVANT SUPPORT.

(1).   /5. (Contd.)

Continued - 2.

5. Plan of Attack - Contd.

No. 15 Platoon in centre. At final Objective will mop up.

No. 16 Platoon will form up in rear of No. 15, and will not advance to final Objective but will mop up, LEVANT TRENCH as already detailed.

6. DOCUMENTS etc.

(a) All bodies which may be found will be stripped of identifications and documents which will be carefully brought back in sandbags to O.C., 'D' Company by those specially detailed.

(b) All dugouts will be thoroughly searched for identifications and documents.

7. PRISONERS.

Prisoners will be sent down BUFFS AVENUE to 'B' Coy. H.Q.

8. SIGNAL for RETURN.

(a) 'C' Company will fire a series of RED Lights on completion of their work.
Each Platoon on their completion of their task will inform Company Headquarters in LEVANT SUPPORT.
As soon as all tasks have been completed 'D' Company Signal will be a series of GREEN lights.
The order to return will be sent to Platoons by runner.

(b) Rifle Grenades bursting into two RED and two WHITE lights will be fired from our Lines to give direction.
A bugle will sound the Regimental Call.

9. WITHDRAWAL.

(a) Care will be taken to return over the same ground and all casualties that may be found will be brought back to our Lines.

(b) After returning to our lines, all men will proceed to Company H.Q. via BUFFS AVENUE and along BEAUMONT RESERVE and report to 2nd. Lieut. COADY.

(c) All runners and Stretcher Bearers will be directed to Battalion and Company Headquarters Aid Post.

Issued at 2-00 p.m. (sgd.) R.W. GOWTHORPE, Capt.
19/7/18.   O.C. - 'D' Company.

Copy No. 1. O.C. - 'C' Coy.
"   " 2. Commanding Officer.
"   " 3.   "
"   " 4. File.

B.M. 1795m

2/R. Ir. Regt.

Reference attached.

1. Appendix 'B' was ommitted as it is presumed you are in possession of a copy.

Appendix 'D' was forwarded to you for perusal before the Raid, when it was explained that there was only one copy of this Appendix in our possession, which was required for the War Diary. This is now forwarded again for perusal and return. If you require a copy of this order, an effort will be made to provide it.

2. Appendix 'E' is also forwarded for your perusal and return. A copy of this will also be provided, if possible, should you require it.

2. The barrages actually fired were those finally decided upon, i.e. as given in your letter attached. The map in the report is the original one provided by the Artillery. This will be cancelled and a revised one forwarded. is now attached

3. In connection with para. 2 above, please note portions marked in Red in enclosed Artillery Order which give the actual lifts adopted.

4. Please return enclosures (Appendices 'D' and 'E') as soon as possible.

5. Reference Raid Report - Section II - PLAN - Appendix 'D' for " 63rd. (RN) Divisional Operation Order No. 208" read " 63rd. (RN) Divisional Artillery Operation Order No. 208. "

H. Steele

Captain,
A/Brigade Major,
188th. Inf. Brigade.

25/7/18.

APPENDIX D - SECTION II - PLAN.

3529
17-7-18
2.35 am

SECRET.

63RD (R.N.) DIVISIONAL ARTILLERY OPERATION ORDER No. 208.
**********oO**********

Headquarters R.A.,
16th July 1918.

1. The 188th Inf. Brigade will carry out a raid on the enemy trenches on the night 19th/20th July 1918.
   FIRST OBJECTIVE. LAVANT Trench from Q.10.b.8.4. to Q.10.b.8.7., including the CRATER.

   SECOND OBJECTIVE. Q.11.a.1.4. to Q.11.a.0.9.

2. The 63rd (R.N.) Divisional Artillery, together with 42nd and 38th D.A's. and V Corps Heavy Artillery, will co-operate according to Table and map attached.
   The C.B.S.O. has also arranged a Counter Battery programme. "Silent" guns will take part.

3. Sufficient ammunition will be dumped beforehand at the guns so that at the end of the operation the normal amount is still on the positions.

4. Artillery Brigade Commanders will please arrange that the nature and extent of hostile Artillery action is recorded and reported to these H.Q. as soon as possible.

5. ZERO HOUR will be notified later.

6. Synchronization of watches will be arranged by Divisional Artillery Signal Officer.

7. At Zero plus 35' 60', fire will cease. Batteries will, however, remain on the line of their last tasks in case of need, until instructed from these H.Q. to resume normal "S.O.S." lines.

8. Wire cutting by the Field Artillery covering the Battalion front is being carried out continuously.
   The Group Commander concerned will obtain the assurance of the Infantry that the wire has been cut to their satisfaction prior to the raid.

9. No mention of this operation is to be made on the telephone.

10. ACKNOWLEDGE. BM 924

G.C. Walford
Major R.A.,
Brigade Major,
63rd (R.N.) Divisional Artillery.

Copies to -
R.A. V Corps.
C.B.S.O., V Corps.
42nd D.A.,
93rd Bde.R.G.A.
188th Inf.Bde.
190th Inf.Bde.
223rd Bde.R.F.A.,
63rd (R.N.) D.A.C.,
O.i/c.Sigs., 33rd D.A.
Rec.Officer,
File.

H.A. V Corps,
63rd (R.N.) Divn.
38th D.A.,
63rd Bn.M.G.C.,
189th Inf.Bde.,
317th Bde.R.F.A.,
232nd Army Bde.R.F.A.,
63rd (R.N.) D.T.M.O.,
Staff Captain,
War Diary,

33RD (B.N.) DIV.ARTY.TASKS.

(To accompany 33rd D.A.Operation Order No.208)

TIME.	UNIT.	TASK.	RATE.	AMN.	REMARKS.
"	"	"	"	"	"
"	"	"	"	"	"
"	"	"	"	"	"
"	"	"	"	"	"
ZERO to Z + 2'.	A/317.	Bombard CRATER from Q.10.b.70.96.— Q.10.b.65.70.	"Rapid".	T.S.	50% on graze.
ZERO to Z + 4'.	A/232.	Bombard from Q.4.d.83.20.to Q.10.b.80.85.	"	"	" See (3 guns on the line of the first shoots(lift,i.o.Q.5.c.10.10.— 2 & 3.(Q.11.a.02.85.
"	B/317.	Bombard from Q.10.b.80.85.to Q.10.b.80.50.	"	"	" (3 guns on the line of the first (lift,Q.11.a.02.85.-Q.11.a.02.50.
"	C/232.	Bombard from Q.10.b.80.50.to Q.10.b.80.15.	"	"	" (3 guns on the line of the first (lift,Q.11.a.02.50.-Q.11.a.00.15.
ZERO onwards.	C/317.	Bombard from Q.4.d.90.20.along NEW BEAUMONT Rd.to Q.5.c.40.05.	"	"	Forms North side of Box barrage.
ZERO onwards.	B/232.	Bombard from Q.10.b.80.15.to Q.10.b.95.14.thence along trench running Easterly to Q.11.a.38.30.	"	"	Forms South side of Box Barrage.
ZERO to Z + 4'.	D/317.	Bombard the line from Q.11.a.10.99.— Q.11.a.10.25.	"	"	H.E.Delay.
Z + 4'to Z + 7'.	"	Lift 100 yards.	"	"	
Z + 7'to Z + 60'.	"	Bombard the line Q.5.c.60.10.to Q.11.a.30.40.to Q.11.a.40.10.	"Normal".	"	
ZERO onwards.	J/232. ½ hows.	Bombard front line from Q.4.d.70.75.-Q.4.d.99.50.— Q.4.d.90.30.	"Rapid"for first 3 mins.then Normal.	H.E.105 fuze. & delay	105 fuze will not be fired S.of Q.4.d.99.50.
ZERO to Z + 5'.	D/232. 2 hows.	Bombard LEVANT Trench at Q.4.d.85.00.	"Rapid".	H.E.delay.	At Z + 5', 2 hows switch those " hows" to front line at Q.4.d.90.30.

Contd........

1.

Sheet 2.   63RD (R.N.) DIV.ARTY.TASKS.

TIME.	UNIT.	TASK.	RATE.	AMM.	REMARKS.
ZERO onwards.	D/223.	Superimposed on task of 4 Hows. of D/232.			
ZERO onwards.	RIGHT GROUP loss D/223.	Bombard (a) from Q.10.d.75.99. to Q.11.c.35.40. (b) Trench from Q.10.d.99.99. to Q.11.c.66.45. (c) Trench from Q.11.c.40.99. to Q.11.c.90.55.	"Rapid" for first 6 mins. then "Normal".	50% T.S. 50% "AX".	
Z + 2' to Z + 60'.	A/317.	Lift and switch on to trench Q.5.c.30.75.—Q.5.c.25.40.	"Normal".	T.S.	
Z + 4' to Z + 7'.		Barrage the line Q.5.c.10.10.— Q.11.a.02.85.			1st lift of 100 yds.
Z + 7' to Z + 9'.	A/252.	Barrage the line Q.5.c.30.05.— Q.11.a.22.85.	"Normal".	T.S.	2nd lift of 100 yds.
Z + 9' to Z + 30'.		Bombard the line Q.5.c.40.10.— Q.11.a.55.85.			3rd lift forming part of E. side of Box Barrage.
Z + 4' to Z + 7'.		Barrage the line Q.11.a.02.85.— Q.11.a.02.50.			1st lift of 100 yds.
Z + 7' to Z + 9'.	B/317.	Barrage the line Q.11.a.22.85.— Q.11.a.20.50.	"Normal".	T.S.	2nd lift of 100 yds.
Z + 9' to Z + 60'.		Bombard the line Q.11.a.35.85.— Q.11.a.35.50.			3rd lift forming part of E.side of Box Barrage.

contd........

Shoot 5.   63RD (R.N.) DIV.ARTY.TASKS.

TIME.	UNIT.	TASK.	RATE.	AMN.	REMARKS.
Z + 4' to Z + 7'.		Barrage the line Q.11.a.02.50.— Q.11.a.00.15.	"Normal".	50% I.S.	1st lift of 100 yds.
Z + 7' to Z + 9'.	O/232.	Barrage the line Q.11.a.20.50.— Q.11.a.20.30.			2nd lift of 100 yds.
Z + 9' to Z + 60'.		Bombard from Q.11.a.35.50. to Q.11.a.35.30.			3rd lift forming part of E. side of Box Barrage.

42ND DIV. ARTY. TASKS.
(To accompany 63rd D.A. Operation Order No.208)

TIME.	NATURE.	TASK.	RATE.	AMMN.	REMARKS.
ZERO onwards	1-18 pr. Bty.	Bombard front line from Q.4.b.70.97.-Q.4.b.55.35.		50%	to guns of each Battery regular lifts as far as
	-do-	From Q.4.b.55.35.-Q.4.d.66.80.	Z to Z + 6': "Rapid". Z + 6' onwards:- "Normal".	50%	
	-do-	Enfilade LIVE ALLEY from Q.4.b.65.15.-Q.5.a.49.05.	"	"	3. The 18 pdr. Bty SMOKE Shell
	-do-	Enfilade LINSEED LANE from Q.5.c.25.90.-Q.5.c.80.77.	"	"	
	1-4.5" How. Bty.	Bombard LINSEED RESERVE from Q.5.c.55.80.-Q.5.c.50.20.	"Normal".	H.E. 106 fuze.	
	1-4.5" How. Bty.	Bombard from Q.S.c.30.85.- Q.S.c.0.5.	"	"	

42ND DIV. ARTY. TASKS.

(To accompany 63rd D.A. Operation Order No.208)

NATURE.	TASK.	TIME.	RATE.	AMN.	REMARKS.
1-18 pr. Bty.	Bombard front line from Q.4.b.70.97.-Q.4.b.55.35.			50% T.S. 50% "AZ".	"After Z plus 6', half the guns of each Battery search forward and back in irregular lifts as far as LINSEED SUPPORT in Q.5.a."
-do-	From Q.4.b.55.-Q.4.d.66.80.	ZERO onwards	Z to Z + 6' :- "Rapid".	"	
-do-	Enfilade LIVE ALLEY from Q.4.b.65.15.-Q.5.a.49.05.		Z + 6' onwards:- "Normal".	"	5. The 18 pdr. Battery enfilading LIVE ALLEY will fire SMOKE Shell.
-do-	Enfilade LINSEED LANE from Q.5.c.25.90.-Q.5.c.80.77.			"	
1-4.5" How. Bty.	Bombard LINSEED RESERVE from Q.5.c.55.80.-Q.5.c.50.20.— Bombard from Q.5.c.30.85.- Q.5.c.0.5.		"Normal".	H.E. 106 fuze.	
1-4.5" How. Bty.			"	"	

38TH (WELSH) DIV. ARTY. TASKS.

(To accompany 63rd D.A. Operation Order No. 208.)

TIME.	UNIT.	TASK.	RATE.	AMN.	REMARKS.
ZERO to Z + 35'.	3-18 pr. Batteries.	Bombard trenches from Q.17.a.95.60.-Q.17.d.35.55.	Z to Z + 6' :- "Rapid". Z + 6' onwards:- "Normal".	50% "A". 50% "A".	"
Z to Z plus 35'.	One 4.5" How. Battery	will make a smoke screen from Q.17.a.10.95. - Q.5.a.95.90.			

HEAVY ARTILLERY TASKS.
(To accompany 63rd Div.Arty.Operation Order No.208)

TIME.	TASK.	NATURE.
ZERO to ZERO + 35'.	Bombard Trench systems in Q.5.a. Trench Junction at Q.5.c.80.80. Sunken Roads and Banks in Q.5.d., Q.11.a & b.	6" Howrs. and 60 pdrs.
Z to Z+60'	STATION Road at Q.11.d.35.85.	8" Howrs.
"	As shown in tracing attached.	"

6" TRENCH MORTARS.

ZERO to ZERO + 35'.	Bombard Q.10.d.95.65. Q.11.c.50.50. Q.5.a.5.. .35.80	"Rapid" first 6 mins. then "Normal."
Z to Z+60'		

****

SECRET.   63rd (RN) M.G. Battalion No. M.G./1212

Amendment No. 3 to Operation Order No. 44.

1. Amendment No. 2 was issued to M.G. Companies and 63rd (RN) Division "G" only. In para. 2, line 3, for Q.6.a.8.2. read Q.8.a.8.2.

2. Cancel para. 2 (c) of Amendment No. 1 and substitute:-

    "Cancel all reference to Zero plus 50 in time and rate of fire columns and substitute to Zero plus 75. In the event of no cease fire signal (Colour to be notified later) having been fired before Zero plus 75 then the barrage will be continued at slow rate until such signal is fired."

18-7-18.   Capt. & Adjt.
                                          for O.C. 63rd (RN) M.G. Battalion.

Copies to:-
    All Recipients of
    O.O. No. 44.

SECRET. APPENDIX E. SECTION II - PLAN   COPY NO. 8

AMENDMENT NO. 1 TO 63RD (RN) M.G. BATTN.   M.G./1178.

OPERATION ORDER NO. 44.

1. Para 2. "C" Company for 8 read 10 guns and amend total to read 54 guns.

2. Para 3. (a) "F" Battery for 8 read 2.

 (b) Insert at end of para:-

Battery Position.	Guns.	Time.	Target.	Rate of fire.	Remarks.
"L" Battery. Q.15.b.6.1.	4.	As for "A" Battery.	Q.11.c.37.60. to Q.11.c.25.80. Searching 350 yards.	As for "A" Battery.	Found by "B" Company. 63rd M.G. Bn.

 (c) Cancel all reference to Zero plus 50 in Time and rate of fire columns and substitute to "Cease Fire" Signal. (Note. The Cease Fire Signal (Colour to be notified later) will be a rifle grenade fired 3 times in succession from our front line trench opposite the point raided. On the last of these grenades being fired the M.G. Barrage will die down).

3. Cancel para 4 and insert - If the situation is clear at 10 minutes after the "cease fire" signal, Batteries will be withdrawn under Unit arrangements.

4. Reference para. 1. The raid will take place on the night 19th/20th July, 1918.

5. Reference para 8. A runner will be despatched to H.Qrs. of Units mentioned in para. 2 at 5-30p.m. on the 19th July.

6. All M.G. Companies, 38th Battalion M.G.C. and 42nd Battalion M.G.C. to acknowledge.

Issued at Noon.
16-7-1918.

T.H.W.Cready
Lieut.Col. R.M.
Commanding 63rd (RN) M.G. Battalion.

Copies to:-

 All Recipients of
 O.O. No. 44.

SECRET.   COPY NO. 7

                                                                       M.G/1174.

           63RD (RN) MACHINE GUN BATTALION OPERATION ORDER NO. 44.

Ref: Map. 57.D/ S.E.
     1/20,000.

1.   At a time and date to be notified later the
        188th Infantry Brigade will raid the trenches marked
        Red in attached tracing.

2.   The following M.G. Units will co-operate:-

        12 Guns.   42nd Battalion M.G.C.
         8 Guns.   "C" Company.)
         8 Guns.   "A" Company.)
         8 Guns.   "B" Company.) 63rd (RN) M.G. Battalion.
         8 Guns.   "D" Company.)(Reserve)
         8 Guns.   36th Battalion M.G.C.

        52 Guns.

3.   The above will have tasks as follows:-

Battery Position.	Guns.	Time.	Target.	Rate of fire.	Remarks.
"A" Battery. To be selected by O.C. 42nd. Battn. M.G.C.	8	Zero. to Zero plus 50	Q.4.b.25.75. to Q.4.b.25.95. searching 500 yards E.	100 R.P.M. for first 5 mins. 75 R.P.M. for next 30 mins. 100 R.P.M. from Zero plus 35 to Zero plus 50.	Found by 42nd BN. M.G.C.
"B" Battery. To be selected by O.C. 42nd. Bn. M.G.C.	4	do	Q.5.a.21.00. to Q.5.a.28.40.	do	do
"C" Battery. Q.3.a.85.45.	4	do	Q.4.b.05.63. to Q.4.b.25.65. searching 500 yards E.	do	Found by "C" Coy. 63rd M.G. Battn.
"D" Battery Q.9.b.6.4.	6	do	Q.4.d.50.88. to Q.5.c.00.45.	do	(1) Guns will be laid direct. (11) Found by "A" Coy.

Battery Position.	Guns.	Time.	Target.	Rate of fire	Remarks.
"E" Battery. Q.2.d.75.70.	6	Zero to Zero plus 50.	Q.4.d.36.20. to Q.4.d.41.50. Enfilading Road 500 yds.	100 R.P.M. for first 5 mins. 75 R.P.M. for next 30 mins. 100 R.P.M. from Zero plus 35 to Zero plus 50.	(i) Guns will be laid direct. (ii) Found by 2 guns "A" Coy. 2 guns "C" Coy. 2 guns "D" Coy.
"F" Battery. Q.3.d.8.6.	8	do	Enfilade N. side of Bank Q.11.a.10.99.	do	(i) Guns will be laid direct. (ii) Found by "C" Coy.
"G" Battery. Q.4.d.05.74.	2	Zero to Zero plus 5.	Trench Q.10.b.85.95.	125 R.P.M.	(i) Guns will be laid direct. (ii) Found by "C" Coy.
"H" Battery. Q.23.a.0.94.	4.	Zero to Zero plus 5.	1st Task. Q.11.a.25.20 to Q.11.a.45.20. Searching N. 400 yards	125 R.P.M.	(i) Found by "B" Coy.
do		Zero plus 7 to Zero plus 50	2nd Task. Q.5.c.3.0. to Q.5.c.5.0. Searching N 500 yards.	75 R.P.M. to Zero plus 35 then 100 R.P.M. to Zero plus 50.	do
"I" Battery. Q.15.a.55.80.	6	As for "A" Battery.	Q.10.d.62.55. to Q.10.d.50.85. Searching 450 yds. N.E.	As for "A" Battery.	Found by "D" Coy.
"J" Battery. To be selected by O.C. 38th Bn. M.G.C.	4	do	Q.11.a.95.60. to Q.11.a.75.85. Searching 250 yds N.E.	do	Found by 38th Bn. M.G.C.
"K" Battery. To be selected by O.C. 38th Bn. M.G.C.	4	do	Q.11.a.95.05 to Q.11.d.2.9.	do	do

4.   At Zero plus 60 if the situation is clear Batteries will be withdrawn under Unit arrangements.

5.   The Left Group Commander is responsible for all detail M.G. arrangements and safety precautions. He will arrange with the Brigade Major, 183th Inf. Bde. to clear any trench in the danger area.

6.   Battery positions will be prepared on the night previous to the raid and all guns will be in position by Zero minus 2 hours.

7.   Sufficient belted ammunition for requirements will be carried in and the empties will be returned to Rear H.Qrs. for refilling immediately after cease fire. Under no circumstances will reserves be depleted.

8.   Orders as to synchronization of watches will be issued later.

9.   M.G. Companies, 38th Battalion M.G.C. and 42nd Battalion M.G.C. to acknowledge.

Issued at midnight,
15/16th July, 1918.

Lieut.Col. R.
Commanding 63rd (RN) M.G. Battn.

Copies to:-

1. 63rd (RN) Division "G".
2. Commanding Officer.
3. Right Group Commander.
4. Left Group Commander.
5. O.C. PURPLE LINE.
6. Reserve Group Commander.
7. 188th Inf. Bde.
8. O.C. Raid.
9. 38th Battalion M.G.C.
10. 42nd Battalion M.G.C.
11. O.M.G.C. V Corps.
12. 63rd (RN) Div. Arty.
13. 2nd Battn. R. Irish Regt.
14. War Diary.
15. War Diary.
16. War Diary.
17. File.
18. Spare.

SECRET.
63rd (RN) M.G. Bn.
Map with O.O.44.
(M.G.1175.)
Ref: 57D SE.
15.6.18.

APPENDIX 'F'.

SECTION III. - EXECUTION. PLAN

188th. L.T.M.BATTERY - ORDER No. 14.

1. **OPERATIONS.**

    The 2nd. Battalion Royal Irish Regt. will carry out a Raid on enemy trenches on night 19/20th. July, 1918.

    188th. L.T.M. Battery will carry out a special firing programme in support of these operations.

    Zero hour will be 12-15 am.

2. **DISPOSITION of T.M. BATTERY.**

    Battery will consist of two Sections.

    (a) <u>No. 1 Section</u>. (Sub.-Lieut. J.A. BEDFORD, R.N.V.R.)
        1 Gun located in disused trench - (Q.10.b.1.4.)

    (b) <u>No. 2 Section</u>. (2/Lieut. W.H. BROWNE)
        7 Guns distributed along bank from Q.4.c.6.7. to)
                                                Q.4.c.8.5.)

    (c) <u>BATTERY HEADQUARTERS</u> (during operations) will be at
                                                Q.4.c.7.6.

3. **TARGETS.**

    (a) <u>No. 1 Section</u> - One gun will fire on 'Y' RAVINE at Q.10.d.6.7 making a demonstration at commencement of operations to take attention from raiding party.

    (b) <u>No. 2 Section</u>.- Three guns will fire on LEVANT TRENCH from Q.4.d.88.00. - northwards to VALLEY.
        Four guns will fire on VALLEY (Q.4.d. and Q.5.c.) fire to be continued until Signal is received that Raiding Party has returned.

4. **RATE of FIRE.**

    (a) <u>No. 1 Section</u>.

        No. 1 Gun. - Zero to Zero plus 4 - 20 rounds
                                                per minute.
    (b) <u>No. 2 Section</u>.

        All Guns. - Zero to Zero plus 10 - 20 rds. per
                                                minute.
        Nos. 2,3,4, & 5 " - Zero plus 10 to Zero plus 30)
                            5 rounds per minute   )

5. **LIGHT SIGNALS.**

    (a) Rifle grenades bursting into two red and two white lights will be sent up during operations to shew raiders direction of line.

    (b) Red and Green Very Lights will be sent up by Companies on completion of allotted tasks.

    (c) White asteroid floating lights will be sent up when all the raiding party has returned.

(1)   /Para. 6.

Contd. - 2.

6. **COMMUNICATION.**

   Communication between Sections and Battery Headquarters and between Battery and Battalion Headquarters will be maintained by runners.

7. **REPORTS.**

   Reports (Ammunition,- Expenditure, Casualties etc.) will be rendered to Battery Headquarters at 4-00 am.

8. **"S.O.S" GUNS.**

   "S.O.S" Guns will be brought from BEAUMONT RESERVE to Advanced Battle Positions after "Stand to" on 19th. inst.
   They will be retained in these positions until after "Stand to" on 20th. inst. when they will be again set up in emplacements in BEAUMONT RESERVE.

9. PLEASE ACKNOWLEDGE.

                                    (Sgd.) R. DONALDSON,
                                           Lieut. R.N.V.R.,
18/7/18.   Cmdg. - 188th. L.T.M. Battery.

Copy No. 11.

OPERATION ORDER No.1/2.

Left Artillery Group.
(63rd (R.N.) Division.)

19th July 18.

With reference to 63rd (R.N.) Divisional Artillery Operation Order No.208, a copy of which with plan on scale of 1/10,000 showing Artillery Barrage is forwarded to all Batteries :-

1. In the opening barrage for A/232, B/317 and C/232 Batteries, half the guns will open on the German Front Line as shown in Sheet 1 of the Table of Tasks, and half will open on the Second Line, i.e. at a lift of 100 yards, these latter guns remaining on this line from Zero to Zero plus 7, the whole ~~hole~~ lifting together at Zero plus 7.

2. In the event of any gun being considered insufficiently reliable for close shooting, it will, from the first fire 200 yards beyond the final barrage line.
    Batteries will report by 12 noon, 19/7/18, the number of guns so dealt with.

3. Artillery fire will continue until Zero plus 60 minutes unless orders to cease firing are received from Group H. Q.
    The order to cease firing will be sent by the code word "PIKE".
    The order to re-open fire, if necessary, will be sent by the code word "CARP". On receipt of this order, Batteries will re-open on their tasks for the final box barrage at rate - one round per gun per minute.

4. In the event of the S. O. S. Signal going up on the Group Front before Zero minus 30 minutes, S. O. S. Fire will be opened.
    Between Zero minus 30 and Zero, S. O. S. Fire will not be opened unless ordered by Group H. Q.
    If the S. O. S. Signal goes up between Zero and Zero plus 60 minutes, Batteries will continue their programme for the raid.

5. Batteries will ensure that correctors are calculated sufficiently long to give 50% on graze. Only ammunition in good condition to be used, and it is to be sorted as carefully as possible.

6. 2/Lieut. E. B. Morley, M.C. (C/232) is detailed as Artillery Liaison Officer with the O. C. Raid. Separate instructions have been issued to him.
    2/Lieut. A. P. Hall, (C/317) is detailed as understudy to 2/Lieut. E. B. Morley.
    2/Lieut. E. B. Morley will report in writing to Group H. Q. by 9 a.m. 20th inst.

7. The Group F. O. O. on duty on the night 19th/20th will be in direct communication with Group H. Q. between Zero minus 15 mins. and Zero plus 60 minutes; between these hours telephone lines in advance of Group H. Q. will be used for tactical messages only.

8. F. O. O. and Batteries will immediately report to Group H. Q. the nature and extent of any hostile fire.

E H Binney

Captain, R. F. A.,
Adjutant, LEFT ARTILLERY GROUP
63rd (R.N.) Division.

Issued at   .

Copy No.1.	A/232.	5. A/317.	9. H.Q., RN Bde.R.F.A.
2.	B/232.	6. B/317.	10. H.Q. 188 Inf. Bde.
3.	C/232.	7. C/317.	11. H.Q. 189 Inf.Bde.

APPENDIX 'G'.

SECTION III - EXECUTION.

Left Artillery Group.
(63rd. (RN) Division.)

Report on Artillery Operations connected with the Raid on night 19th./20th. July.

1. **PREPARATORY.** The area to be raided having been decided on on 10/7/18, wire cutting commenced on 11/7/18 and was continued daily up to the day of the raid. Two 4.5" Howitzer Batteries (D/232 and D/317) firing 106 fuzes, were employed for this, and two 6" T.Ms. of Y/63rd. T.M.B.

   In order not to attract special attention to the area to be raided, wire cutting was simultaneously carried out in Q.10.d. and Q.4.b. and d.

   During the same time, known and suspected M.G. emplacements from which fire could be directed on to the raiding area and jumping off place, were systematically bombarded by 4.5" Howitzers and T.Ms., special attention being paid to the localities about Q.10.b.8.8., Q.4.d.9.0., the CRATER, Q.4.d.9.6. Q.11.a.05.50. and Q.10.b.90.15.

   The wire South and East of the CRATER being invisible from our Lines, both 4.5" Howitzer Batteries successfully registered it with aeroplane observation, and similarly B/232 (18 pdr. Battery) successfully registered the trench Q.4.b.90.15.

   A proportion of ammunition was expended on wire cutting at night.

   The Infantry Patrol reports on wire were passed to the Artillery group Commander daily and formed the basis for subsequent wire-cutting programmes.

   After wire-cutting, 4.5" Howitzer and 18 pdr. fire was directed on the locality intermittently at night.

2. **CONFERENCES.** The Group Commander attended conferences at the H.Q. of the O.C., Raiding Battalion on 14th. and 17th.
   At these Conferences, the details of Infantry and Artillery action were determined, and detailed plans were subsequently drawn up.

3. **LIAISON.** 2/Lieut. E.B. MORLEY, M.C., Artillery Liaison Officer with O.C., Raid, took up his duties on 14/7/18, and kept the O.C., Raid, informed as to progess in wire-cutting and passed suggestions of O.C., Raid to the Group Commander.

4. **PRACTICE RAIDS.** The Group Commander was present at two practice Raids carried out by the Raiding Party, and gave effect to certain minor alterations there decided on, including timing of the barrage,

5. **ARTILLERY PROGRAMME.** The Artillery Programme for the raid is shewn in the attached orders. The arrangements made for the raid were embodied in 63rd. (RN) Divisional Artillery Operation Order No. 208 dated 16/7/18.

   Field Artillery selected for the close support of the Raid consisted of the Left Artillery Group with B/232

/ Battery

Contd. - 2.

Para. 5 - Contd.

B/232/ Battery of the Right Artillery Group: a total of 6- 18-pdrs Batteries and 2 4.5." How. Batteries.

The programme consisted of a creeping barrage opening on the CRATER and the German Front Line, and lifting and resting on trenches and emplacements, and finally forming the back side of a box barrage 150 to 200 yards beyond the furthest point of raid.

The sides of the Box Barrage were formed by 2 18-pdr. Batteries firing in enfilade and opening at Zero hour.

Registration was carried out with a minimum number of rounds, and two worn 18-pdr. guns were allotted tasks well over the final barrage line.

6. HEAVY ARTILLERY. The action of Heavy Artillery and 42nd. and 38th. Divisional Artilleries is shewn on attached plan.

7. MAINTAINANCE OF FIRE. The Artillery Programme was carried out as arranged, but fire was maintained until Zero plus 85, at the request of the O.C., Raid.

8. COMMUNICATIONS. The Liaison Officer with O.C., Raid established telephone and visual communications with Group H.Q. from the Front Line Trench and excellent communication was maintained througout the Raid.

9. BARRAGE TABLES. The Barrage Tables reached Battery Commanders concerned 30 hours before Zero hour, giving them ample time for preparation.

10. MAPS. In making preparations for a raid a good supply of flimsy maps of the raid area is of great assistance to the Artillery; Artillery Brigades have no facilities for making these maps.

          (Sgd) M. TOVEY,
           Lieut.- Colonel, R.F.A.
       Commanding LEFT ARTILLERY GROUP,
21st. July, 1918.   63rd. (RN) Division.

TRACE TO ACCOMPANY LEFT GROUP ARTY ORDER.

PART OF SHEET 57D S.E.   SCALE 1:10,000

APPENDIX 'H'.

SECTION III. - EXECUTION.

Report on Machine Gun Action in Raid on night of 19th/20th. July.

1. 54 Machine Guns were detailed to support the Raid.
   A Box Barrage was placed round the area raided, and in addition 4 guns fired direct on the Left Flank.

2. All guns opened immediately the Artillery Barrage had got well going - this was about Zero plus 10 Seconds. Fire was continued during the whole period until Zero plus 90, when, on the Signal going up, fire ceased.

3. Enemy Artillery retaliation was slight.

4. Number of rounds fired - approx. 300,000.

(Sgd.) J. LIGHTBODY,
Captain,
O.C. - Left Group - 63rd.(RN) Div.
M.G. Battalion.

21/7/18.

APPENDIX I.

SECTION III - EXECUTION.

Report on Special Operations in connection with Raid by 2nd. Royal Irish Regiment on night 19th/20th. July.

1. **OPERATIONS.**

    2nd. Battalion Royal Irish Regt. carried out a Raid on enemy trenches on night 19th./20th.

    188th. L.T.M. Battery fired 936 rounds in support of these operations.

2. **DISPOSITION OF BATTERY.**

    1 gun was located in disused trench - at Q.10.b.1.4.

    7 guns were distributed along Bank from Q.4.c.6.7. to Q.4.c.8.5.

3. **ZERO-HOUR**

    Zero hour was 12-15 a.m.

    Trench Mortar Battery opened fire with first rounds of Artillery Barrage.

4. **TARGETS.**

    73 rounds were fired on 'Y' RAVINE at Q.10.d.6.7. with a view to taking attention from the Raiding party.

    863 rounds were fired on LEVANT TRENCH from Q.4.d.86.00. Northwards to the VALLEY and also on the Valley (Q.4.d. and Q.5.c.) Rapid fire was carried out from 12-15 am. to 12-25 am., the guns firing on the VALLEY continuing thereafter until 12-40 am.

5. **CASUALTIES.**

    1 Other Rank was wounded while serving his mortar.

6. **ENEMY FIRE.**

    Enemy retaliation was not heavy in the neighborhood of L.T.M. positions, and did not open until 3 minutes after Zero hour.

    One Machine Gun enfiladed bank (Q.4.d.) from about Q.10.d.6.7.

20/7/18.

(Sgd.) R. DONALDSON,
Lieutenant. R.N.V.R.
Cmdg. - 188th. L.T.M. Battery.

SECTION III.

EXECUTION.

1. **Forming up.**

    Raiding troops were lined out according to plan by zero minus 15 minutes. The assembly was carried out in good order and according to time table.
    Opinions differ as to whether the enemy detected the forming up; rifle and Machine Gun shots were directed towards the troops, but there were no casualties.

2. **COURSE of EVENTS.**

    Artillery and Machine Gun barrages opened punctually at Zero, synchronization being good. The general opinion of the Raiders is that the barrages were very good and accurate and well planned Immediately the barrages commenced, the raiding troops crawled forward as near to the barrage as possible, and then rushed the enemy's Front Line directly the barrage lifted.

    Action of 'D' Company.

    It had been anticipated that a hostile Machine Gun would be found in a sap at about Q.10.b.7.3. and a special party under Sergeant FAGAN was detailed to deal with this eventuality. As expected the gun was found in position but was quickly overcome by Sergeant FAGAN'S party which was skilfully handled. This obstacle cleared, LEVANT TRENCH was entered without much opposition.

    The Company then pressed on towards LEVANT SUPPORT TRENCH and met with heavy opposition from several Machine Guns East of the CRATER, between the two trenches. Only portions of 'D' Company eventually reached LEVANT SUPPORT owing to enfilade fire from about Q.10.b.85.80. Despite this, however, several dugouts were bombed. The Company was then withdrawn after a search for 'C' Company on the Left had failed, the last man to return to our lines being Captain GOWTHORPE, O.C., Company, who did excellent work in the withdrawal.

    Action of 'C' Company.

    'C' Company met with a more formidable resistance and during its advance suffered casualties from Machine Guns firing from about Q.10.b.85.80.
    The CRATER itself and the portion of LEVANT TRENCH just South of it were captured, but during this operation Captain PIKE, his Subaltern Lieut. CHIVERS, and several N.C.Os. became casualties, and from that time onwards little progress was made, and only a few men reached LEVANT SUPPORT.

    Several dugouts East of the Southern portion of the CRATER however, were successfully bombed.

    The withdrawal of this Company was premature owing to the fact that the men mistook lights sent up by the enemy for those decided on by the Officers Commanding Raiding Companies to indicate to one another that they were ready to withdraw.

    The CRATER shewed no sign of occupation except for one bombing post about Q.10.b.70.75.; There were no signs of any attempt to open up gallery leading into our Lines.

3. **Casualties.**

    Casualties were as under :-

OFFICERS.			OTHER RANKS.			TOTAL.		
Killed.	Wounded.	Missing.	Killed.	Wounded.	Missing.	Killed.	W'ded.	Miss'g.
-	2.	-	3	27	8	3	29	8

Total Casualties - 40

(1). /para. 4.

Contd. - 2.

4. **Losses inflicted on Enemy.**

    (a) 1 Machine Gun, 4 O.Rs. captured. (2 more O.Rs. were captured but were killed on the way to our lines)

    (b) 25 O.Rs. killed - all by bombs and Rifle fire. Large numbers were seen running away, the majority of whom must have been killed by our Artillery fire.

    Numbers wounded not known.

    (c) A number of dugouts bombed.

5. **Enemy Action.**

    (a) The enemy, as usual, made use of a great number of Light Signals which were sent up directly over the area raided (but nowhere else), as soon as the Front attacked became clearly defined.

    (b) The enemy's barrage started about Zero plus 5 minutes, and lasted until our barrage ceased, when it stopped almost simultaneously. It was never heavy. 77 mm. shelled enemy's own wire. 150 mm. shelled South of BUFF'S AVENUE and on Right of the Brigade Sector between BEAUMONT RESERVE and the Front Line

    (c) The enemy used a number of bombs but there was very little Rifle fire, all riflemen apparently getting into dugouts directly our barrage opened and leaving the defence to Machine Gunners.

    (d) As usual, the backbone of the enemy's defence was his Machine Guns. Active guns were located as follows :-

    No. 1 at Q.10.b.78.65.   (Team killed - gun not removed)

    No. 2 at Q.10.b.83.70.   (Team - 1 killed, 1 captured, gun not removed).

    No. 3. at Q.10.b.85.80. - Silenced.

    No. 4.)   about   )
    No. 5.) Q.10.b.90.85.)   Remained in action.

    No. 6. at Q.10.b.7.3.   Captured by Sergeant FAGAN with team of 2 men.

    In all cases these Machine Guns were surrounded with barbed wire.

    (e) Enemy 'S.O.S' Rocket - Double Green - repeated to the rear.

21/7/18.

(Sgd.) M.C.C. HARRISON
Lieut-Colonel,
Commanding -
2nd. Battn.- Royal Irish Regiment.

SECTION IV.

NOTES and LESSONS.

1. ENEMY PREPAREDNESS.

It appears that the enemy were fully prepared for a raid on the Brigade Front, and seemed to expect it on the night it took place. From 11 p.m., when one of our Patrols approached his line, onwards, an abnormal number of Very Lights were fired along the Front; our Front Line was occasionally swept by Machine Gun and Rifle fire (an exceptional occurrence), and at one time the enemy bombed his own wire.

The forming up was quietly done, but the troops were fired on, so it is possible that movement was detected. Directly our barrage opened, the enemy sent up 2 Green Lights (S.O.S. Signal), but the hostile Artillery did not reply until Zero plus 5 minutes.

On the other hand there is no doubt that the enemy is constantly on the alert, especially as wire-cutting has been proceeding for the last week or ten days along the front, and that he has been frequently raided lately.

2. ARTILLERY and MACHINE GUN BARRAGES.

These were very good and accurate. The rate of the Infantry advance was overestimated however. In many cases our men did not keep up with the barrage and this undoubtedly enabled the enemy to get his Machine Guns in action against them and resulted in casualties. A pause was required in the first objective to re-organize the troops for an advance on to the 2nd. objective. It is thought that the pause should have been for 10 minutes, which would have meant that the Artillery barrage should have 'stood' on the 2nd. Objective 4 Zero plus 14 minutes before lifting.

For further details see reports of O.C., 232nd. Brigade R.F.A. and O.C. Left Group - 63rd. (RN) Machine Gun Battalion - Appendices 'G' and 'H' of Section III - ~~PLAN~~. EXECUTION.

3. PLAN OF ATTACK.

Events proved that reports received from Patrols and observers were accurate. The Western edge of the CRATER was not held and was not wired. The Eastern edge, however, was well wired (the only wire on the whole front uncut) and held. For this reason a frontal attack through the CRATER would have been very difficult, as the attackers would have been obliged to climb out of the CRATER up a steep slope and through wire in face of opposition. It is thought, therefore, that the original plan of taking the CRATER from the South gave the best chances of success, and I consider it would have succeeded had not the Company Officers and N.C.Os. of 'C' Company become casualties at a critical time, and had the chain of Command after their loss been strong enough to organize attacks for the capture of the Machine Guns which held up the attack.

4. COMMUNICATIONS.

(i) The tracer ammunition used to define the flanks of the attack proved of great assistance.

(ii) It was a mistake to use Very Lights to shew that Companies had completed their tasks, as the enemy used similar lights, and in consequence, confused the raiders.

(1)   /Para. 4 (iii)

Contd. - 2.

Para. 4 - Contd.

    (iii) The bugle calls used as a guide for the raiders towards their own lines proved useful.

    (iv) The old S.O.S. Signal (Rifle Grenade bursting into 2 Red and 2 White Lights) fired at intervals of 3 minutes from our lines, to shew the raiders the way back, also proved useful ; a large supply is necessary.

    (v) Signals from Raid Headquarters rearwards worked excellently.

    (vi) The Raiding Companies took no wires with them.

    (vii) A Runner was sent back to Raid Headquarters by both Company Commanders. Neither arrived as both were wounded en route.

5. ORGANIZATION OF RAID.

    The Raid, which was a large one, took place while the Battalion was in the Advanced Forward Zone, and a great deal of difficulty was found in organizing the raiding parties, before the raid, and still more in re-organizing them after their return while in the forward trenches.
    To avoid these difficulties the following procedure is suggested :-

    The unit selected for the raid should do a tour in the trenches, during which period the objective should be reconnaitred and 'No Man's Land' learnt by the Raiders. The Unit should then be withdrawn into Reserve when practices should take place, and then moved direct to the Front Line and carry out the Raid on the same night or day, moving through the troops holding the Front Line to do so. This done, the Raiders should move back direct to their positions in Reserve.

6. USE OF L.T.M. BATTERY.

    The bulk of the L.T.M. Battery was used to thicken up the Box Barrage on the Left Flank, North of the CRATER. To judge by events, it would have been better, it appears, to have employed it against the Eastern edge of the CRATER, where its high angled fire might possibly have dealt with Machine Guns hidden behind the CRATER debris, which the field guns with their flat trajectory could not touch.
    For further details see report of O.C., 188th. L.T.M. Battery - Appendix - Section III. - PLAN. EXECUTION.

7. DESTRUCTION OF DUGOUTS.

    The 'P' Bombs - No. 27 were not a success in destroying dugouts. They do not burn the wood-work and only make a great deal of smoke, which does not inconvenience the inhabitants provided they are not near the dugout entrance and put on their gas masks.
    I consider that it would have been better to have sent over a detachment of R.E. with the Infantry, provided with special charges. This would have ensured the distruction of dugouts.

/Para. 8.

Contd. - 3.

8. **USE OF RIFLES.**

   The Raiders made very little use of rifle fire, even when numbers of the enemy were seen running away.

9. **USE OF No. 5. MILLS BOMBS.**

   A number of bombs were used for bombing dugouts and Machine Guns (in the latter case 3 times successfully. There was a certain amount of promiscuous bombing when rifle fire would have been more effective.

10. **RIFLE BOMBS.**

    These were not used. It is difficult to get accurate shooting out of these weapons by day, and this, it is considered would be accentuated at night when the position of our troops and the enemy was not properly known. Rifle Bombs might, however, prove useful if used by troops employed on flank guards.

11. **MEDICAL ARRANGEMENTS.**

    Medical arrangements were as good as could be expected. Getting the wounded down dugouts for dressing proved very difficult, and the usual difficulty of carrying men down Communication Trenches was apparent.
    Stretcher Cases took from 2 to 2½ hours to reach the Advanced Dressing Station from the Front Line.

12. **FLANK GUARDS.**

    The left flank guard did useful work and engaged hostile Machine Guns with its Lewis Guns. The right flank, after the Machine Gun at Q.10.b.7.3. was captured was not menaced ; the enemy made no attempt to leave their cover in 'Y' Ravine.

21/7/18.   (Sgd.) M.C.C. HARRISON,
                                                   Lieut-Colonel,
21/7/18.   Commanding -
                                            2nd. Battn. - Royal Irish Regiment.

"C" Form.
MESSAGES AND SIGNALS.

Army Form C. 2123.
(In books of 100.)

Prefix **BM** Code **H1AF** Words **8**

From **WULA**
By **Moulan**

Office Stamp: **MOSI 20/4/18**

Handed in at **WULA** Office **6.45** m. Received **8.55** m.

TO **MOSI**

*Sender's Number	Day of Month	In reply to Number	AAA
BM	20	—	
	Well done	MOSI	

FROM / TIME & PLACE: **WULA**

"C" Form.

MESSAGES AND SIGNALS.

Army Form C. 2123.
(In books of 100.)
No. of Message..........

Prefix...SM... Code...11AM... Words...95...
Received. From WULA
By Mushon

Sent, or sent out.
At..........m.
To..........
By..........

Office Stamp.
MOSI
20/7/18

Charges to Collect
Service Instructions.

Handed in at......WULA...... Office 9.45 a/m. Received 9.49 a.m.

TO   MOSI

*Sender's Number	Day of Month	In reply to Number	AAA
BM 18	20th		

The GOC has much pleasure in forwarding the following +++ Begins +++ GEN BYNG congratulates MOSI on raid Ends +++

FROM TIME & PLACE   WULA

*This line should be erased if not required.

B.M. 1868.

2/R. Ir. Regt.

  The attached letter is forwarded for your information.

  The General Officer Commanding is very pleased with the result of your Raid.

        H. Steele
          Captain,
          A/Brigade Major,
31/7/18.   188th. Inf. Brigade.

V Corps No. GS.456/11.

G.O.C.,
R.N.Division.

Many congratulations on your successful raid. Please thank the 188th Infantry Brigade and the 2/Royal Irish Regiment for the careful plans and hard fighting which resulted in the destruction of a large number of Boches.

The 2/Royal Irish Regiment need have no doubt of their being able to beat Germans whenever they meet them.

                                        Sd.   C.D.SHUTE,
20-7-18.   Lieutenant General

-2-

63rd (RN) Division No.GA.5/30.

188th Infantry Brigade.

The above congratulatory letter from V Corps Commander has just been received by Special D.R.

                                          Lieutenant Colonel,
                                          General Staff.
20-7-18.   3   63rd (RN) Division.

The 2nd Royal Irish Regiment

I am very pleased and proud to be able to forward the above. I heartily agree with para 2 of the Corps Commander's note, and hope you will set about planning another enterprise for the discomforture of the enemy in the future.

                                      J.D. Coleridge, Brig Gen.
20-7-1918.   Commanding 188th Bde.

B.O. File Appendix No. 8   Copy No 9

1. The 2nd Lincoln Regt will relieve the 2nd R.I. Regt in the Purple System on night 24/25th July.

2. Guides 1 per platoon, 1 per Coy H.Q & 1 Battn H.Q to be at P.12 & K.10 by 9.30 pm.

3. All trench stores, reserve water, ammunition, defensive schemes etc to be carefully handed over & receipts obtained. Spare [?] lines will also be handed over.

4. On completion of relief the Battalion will move to billets in LEALVILLERS. All movement to be by platoons at a distance 200 yards apart. Routes to be reconnoitred under Coy arrangements. Tracks will be used unless the weather is bad.

5. On 25th Battn will proceed to billets in RAINCHEVAL vacated by 2nd Lincolns. H.Q moving off at 8 am. A Coy 8.5 am. B. 8.10 am C 8.15 am. D 8.20. An interval of 200 yards to be kept between companies. All units will have a ten minute halt regularly at ten minutes to each hour.

6. Transport

(a) The transport will take over lines [?] occupied by Lincolns on morning of 24th. A representative to be left [?]

over present lines to Lindenhoek.

~~Rations~~

(b) 2 Limbers per Coy. 1 for Battn H.Q. Maltese Cart & Mess Cart to be at Coy & Battn H.Q. by 10 pm on night 24th. These limbers will dump rations at Lealvillers. C.Q.M.S remaining there.
~~Breakfasts on 25th to be served at 7 am~~
Cookers will proceed as far as Lealvillers.
~~Cookers will~~

(c) Breakfasts on 25th to be served at 7 am.
Limbers remain returning from Purple system with L.G's will remain at Lealvillers till Coys move off on 25th.
Limbers containing petrol tins & kits will proceed direct to transport lines at ~~RAINNEVAL~~
N.11.d.4.2.

(7) Relief complete in Purple system to be notified by Code word "TINS"

(8) Billeting parties
Advanced billeting party under ~~~~ Sanderson will meet the Acty Staff Captain at the Town Major's Office Lealvillers at 12 noon on 24th inst.
 to meet the Staff Captain at town major's office RAINNEVAL at 2 pm 24 inst.

3.

All Trench stores, defence scheme etc to be carefully handed over & receipts obtained. Ammunition in C.T's to be shown on a different list to ammunition in localities.

Advanced billeting party under Lt Sanderson to meet a/g Staff Captain at Town Major's office, RAINCHEVAL at 9 am on 25th inst.

Surplus battle personnel & reinforcements to be included in billeting returns.

All troops at present at transport lines will move to RAINCHEVAL on morning 24th inst. To be employed in digging out transport lines, improving billets etc.

      Sd R.T. Hamilton 2/Lieut & Adjt
                          7th R. Irish Regt

Issued at 10.30 pm.
Copies to

1. HQ 188 Bde
2. OC of Lincolns
3. OC A Coy
4. " B "
5. " C "
6. " D "
7. All Offrs comd @ Tpt Lines
8. RSM
9. File

Appendix No. 9
Copy No. 14

2ND. RL. IRISH REGT.   DEFENCE SCHEME   (PROVISIONAL).

1. In addition to being in G.H.Q. Reserve, the 63RD. DIV. is Div. in CORPS RESERVE.

2. Troops of 188th. Inf. Bde. will be prepared to move:-
   (a) At one hour's notice from 9 pm - 9 am. daily.
   (b) At two hours notice from 9 am - 9 pm daily.

3. The Bde. is disposed as follows:-

   Bde H.Q. – ST. LEGER.   R. M. Bn. – AUTHIE.
   ANSON Bn – AUTHIE.   RL. IRISH – ST. LEGER.
   T. M. B – ST. LEGER.

4. In the event of attack the 188th. Bde. will be prepared to carry out any of the following duties:-

   Duty No. 1 On receipt of the order "BATTLE STATIONS A" from Bde. H.Q. Units will assemble in positions of readiness for counter-attack in the ROSSIGNOL FARM Valley in J. 3. a., b., and c.

   Duty No. 2. On receipt of the order "BATTLE STATIONS "B" Units will assemble in a positions of readiness for counter-attack about the COUIN Valley in J. 2. a., and b.

   Duty No. 3. To counter-attack within the IV Corps Area to restore any part of the PURPLE LINE or COLINCAMPS – MAILLY MAILLET Switch that may be penetrated.

   Duty No. 4. In the event of a break-through on our left to counter-attack in the VI Corps Area.

   Duty No. 5. In the event of a break-through on our right to counter-attack in the V Corps Area.

Details of the above duties will be issued as Appendices to this Defence Scheme.

5. **PROTECTION**   After receipt of the order "BATTLE STATIONS", Units will never move without proper protection by Advanced and Flank Guards.

6. INTERVALS. 100 yds. intervals between Companies; 50 yds. between Platoons by night to be increased by day according to circumstances.

7. CONTACT AEROPLANES: Should Aeroplanes call for flares during operations when none are in possession of the men, they will shew their position to the 'planes by waving helmets, etc

Tilney Capt. & Adjt.
of R.I. Regt.

Distribution:
- No. 1 H.Q. 188 Bde.
- 2. Sec. in Command.
- 3. O/C A Coy
- 4. "   B "
- 5. "   C "
- 6. "   D "
- 7. M.O.
- 8. Q.M.
- 9. I.O.
- 10. L.G.O.
- 11. Asst. Adjt.
- 12. R.S.M.
- 13. Sig. Sergt.
- 14. File
- 15. War Diary
- 16. 17. 18. Spare

Copy No 18

2ND. RL. IRISH REGT. DEFENCE SCHEME (PROVISIONAL)

1. In addition to being in G.H.Q. Reserve, the 63RD. DIV. is DIV. in CORPS RESERVE.

2. Troops of 188th Inf. Bde. will be prepared to move:-
   (a) At one hour's notice from 9 pm - 9 am. daily.
   (b) At two hours notice from 9 am - 9 pm daily.

3. The Bde. is disposed as follows:-

   Bde H.Q. - ST. LEGER.   R.M. Bn. - AUTHIE.
   ANSON Bn - AUTHIE.   RL. IRISH - ST. LEGER.
   T.M.B - ST. LEGER.

4. In the event of attack the 188th Bde. will be prepared to carry out any of the following duties:-

   Duty No. 1. On receipt of the order "BATTLE STATIONS A" from Bde. H.Q. Units will assemble in positions of readiness for counter-attack in the ROSSIGNOL FARM Valley in J.3. a., b., and c.

   Duty No. 2. On receipt of the order "BATTLE STATIONS B" Units will assemble in a positions of readiness for counter-attack about the COUIN Valley in J.2. a., and b.

   Duty No. 3. To counter-attack within the IV Corps Area to restore any part of the PURPLE LINE or COLINCAMPS - MAILLY MAILLET Switch that may be penetrated.

   Duty No. 4. In the event of a break-through on our left to counter-attack in the VI Corps Area.

   Duty No. 5. In the event of a break-through on our right to counter-attack in the V Corps Area.

   Details of the above duties will be issued as Appendices to this Defence Scheme.

5. **PROTECTION** After receipt of the order "BATTLE STATIONS", Units will never move without proper protection by Advanced and Flank Guards.

2

6. INTERVALS.   100 yds. intervals between Companies;
50 yds. between Platoons by night to be
increased by day according to circumstances.

7. CONTACT AEROPLANES: Should Aeroplanes call for
flares during operations when none are in
possession of the men, they will shew their
position to the planes by waving helmets, etc.

Capt. & Adjt.
R. 1. Regt.

Distribution:
    No. 1   H.Q. 188 Bde.
    2.   Sec. in Commd.
    3.   O/C A Coy
    4.   " B "
    5.   " C "
    6.   " D "
    7.   M.O.
    8.   Q.M.
    9.   I.O.
    10. L.G.O.
    11. Asst. Adjt.
    12. R.S.M.
    13. Sig. Sergt.
    14. File
    15. War Diary
  16. 17. 18. Spare

2 R Irish Rgt
Vol 41
Appx

1918

201.
(12 sheets)

WAR DIARY
INTELLIGENCE SUMMARY.

Army Form C. 2118.

Place	Date	Hour	Summary of Events and Information	Remarks and references to Appendices
ST. LEGER	1918 Aug 1		Battalion in G.H.Q. Reserve. Reconnaissance of Line and parties.	
	- 4		Generally in attached positions in COIGNEUX VALLEY. Battalion transferred from V Corps to IV Corps.	
	4		The Officer A.C.O. was relieved by 16th (S) W. Coast Coy 2nd Wellington Regiment. War Establishment by the Battalion.	
			Battalion rejoins V Corps and moves to LOUVENCOURT.	
LOUVENCOURT	5	2 PM	Battalion moves at 2 p.m. to junction to ACHEUX WOOD	
	8		Cricket match 2nd Rutland Irish Regt -v- 2nd Wellington Regt. Result - win to 2nd Rutland Irish Regt by 9 runs.	
		8 PM	Battalion moves to CONTAY and joins III Corps IV Army.	
CONTAY	8-14		Battalion at CONTAY training.	
	15		Battalion rejoins IV Corps III Army and moves to HENU WOOD.	
HENU	16-19		Battalion Training.	

WAR DIARY
or
INTELLIGENCE SUMMARY.

Army Form C. 2118.

Place	Date	Hour	Summary of Events and Information	Remarks and references to Appendices
HENU	1918 Augt 19	10 AM	Battalion in Camp West of HENU. Conference for all C.O.s at Div H.Q when operation orders issued	See Appendix No. 1
		1 PM	Reconnaissance of assembly position	
		10 P.M	Battalion moves to Tape Line East of SOUASTRE.	
	20	11.45 P.M.	Moves to Assembly position 1 mile East of ESSARTS (between BRADFORD and HALIFAX Trenches.	
	21	4.55 A.M.	Attack commences. Regt. 1 with Battalion Lewis Guns. Battn. Scouts N. & ABLAINZEVILLE — LOG EAST used to capture final Objective Railway cutting West of ACHIET-LE-GRAND. Owing to dense fog great difficulty was experienced in keeping direction later (?) before about 10 AM some of centre & Eastern flank Battalion was obliged to consolidate line about 500 yards from final objective. 70 prisoners & 8 M.G was being been captured by Battn.	

Army Form C. 2118.

WAR DIARY
or
INTELLIGENCE SUMMARY.
(Erase heading not required.)

Place	Date	Hour	Summary of Events and Information	Remarks and references to Appendices
	1918			
	Aug 21	9 PM	Patrol of Lieut GIFFIN captured 8 Germans & 1 M.Gun on Eastern side of Railway	
			Casualties A/Capt R.W. GOWTHORPE M.C. – Wounded	
			Lieut. W.F. SLAVIN (A.S.C.) – "	
			A/Capt. R.E.W. BURKE M.C. "	
			2nd Lieut A. GORMAN "	
			" J. COADY (Con. Rangers) – Killed	
			20 O.R. – Killed	
			115 " – Wounded	
			80 " – Missing	
	22	1.30 PM	Line captured on 21st successfully held against several local counter attacks. Enemy succeeded in entering Trenches by Royal Fusiliers but were at once driven out by a party of Royal Irish led by Lieut. WARREN	
			Casualties 2 O.R. – Killed	
			30 " – Wounded	Loss
			5 " – Missing	

WAR DIARY
or
INTELLIGENCE SUMMARY.

(Erase heading not required.)

Army Form C. 2118.

Instructions regarding War Diaries and Intelligence Summaries are contained in F. S. Regs., Part II. and the Staff Manual respectively. Title pages will be prepared in manuscript.

Place	Date	Hour	Summary of Events and Information	Remarks and references to Appendices
	1918			
	Aug 23	2 AM	Line held by 63rd divn is taken over by Inf. Bde & Batts withdrawn to return in all German front line Trench immediately East of ABLAINZEVILLE — LOGEAST wood — heavy gas shelled during the relief	
	24	5 AM	188th Lf. Brigade concentrates at NW corner of LOGEAST Wood. Brigade were to attack THILLOY LA BARQUE for ridge where LOUPART WOOD GREVILLERS Attack to commence at 7.30 P.M. but postponed after Brigade was formed up	

(A7883) Wt W869/M1672 350,000 4/17 **Sch. 52a** Forms/C/2118/14

WAR DIARY
or
INTELLIGENCE SUMMARY.
(Erase heading not required.)

Army Form C. 2118.

Place	Date	Hour	Summary of Events and Information	Remarks and references to Appendices
	1918 Aug 25	5 AM	Attack on THILLOY — LA BARQUE launched under cover of heavy mist. R. Marine Batt. on right, ANSON and R. Fus. Capts on left. All objectives captured but subsequent counter attack on THILLOY when mist lifted enabled the enemy to recapture the village. Our own party on Eastern outskirts of village fighting to last man. A line running West of THILLOY through LIGNY THILLOY and 800x LA BARQUE was successfully held by Ka Brigade. The Royal Irish on the extreme left being in touch with the 2ⁿᵈ Batt. of 7th/10th Wellington West Coast Regt. Enemy the operation 8 Officers 100 O.R. x 10 M Guns were captured by Ka Battalion. Casualties. 2ⁿᵈ Lieut. J.E. LOWRY — Killed. " W.R. SIMMONS — Missing A/Capt. R.T. HAMILTON MC — Wounded 2ⁿᵈ Lieut W. CROFT — " " E.G. WILSON — " 18 O.R — Killed 65 " — Wounded 41 " — Missing	

WAR DIARY
or
INTELLIGENCE SUMMARY.

Army Form C. 2118.

(Erase heading not required.)

Place	Date	Hour	Summary of Events and Information	Remarks and references to Appendices
	1918 Aug 26	7 AM	Brigade launched a Counter attack on THILLOY. This village and high ground to North were found to be very strongly held by Machine Gun posts and our troops were eventually forced to withdraw to their former line. Casualties A/Capt B.J. GLANCY M.C. — Wounded Lieut O. CROSBIE — " 3 O.R. — Killed 18 " — Wounded	
	27		Attacks at 11 A.M. & 6 P.M. by 190 Brigade on THILLOY both repulsed by M.Gun fire. 63rd Div. relieved by 42nd Div.	
MIRAUMONT	28	11:30 P.M.	On relief by 5th Manchester Regt. Battn. withdraws to sunk road West of MIRAUMONT	A+C

WAR DIARY or INTELLIGENCE SUMMARY.

Army Form C. 2118.

Place	Date	Hour	Summary of Events and Information	Remarks and references to Appendices
MIRAUMONT	198 May 30	11.50 P.M.	Div. is transferred to XVII CORPS and Battalion moves to BOIRY STE - RICTITUDE.	
			HONOURS & AWARDS CAPT. I.E. ST.J. PIKE — Bar to M.C.	
			Lt N.M.T.H. CHEVERS — M.C.	
			A/CAPT. R.W. GOWTHORPE — "	
			C.Q.M.S. DONOVAN — D.C.M.	
			L/CPL DUFFELL M.M. D.C.M	
			SERGT WATSON D.C.M — "	
			" GATES — "	
			" ADAMS — "	
			CORPL CARBERRY — "	
			and seven other awards of Military Medals.	

WAR DIARY

INTELLIGENCE SUMMARY.

(Erase heading not required.)

Army Form C. 2118.

Place	Date	Hour	Summary of Events and Information	Remarks and references to Appendices
	1918 Aug. 1		REINFORCEMENTS OFFICERS	
			CAPT D. FOULKES	
			" R. BLACKETT (S.L.H.)	
			LIEUT N MANLY	
			2/LT M. LAWLER	
			" E.S. HUNTER	
			" W. McCREEDY	
			and 250 OTHER RANKS.	

T Hughes for Lieut. Colonel
Commanding 2nd The Royal Irish Regt.

Army Form C. 2118.

WAR DIARY
or
INTELLIGENCE SUMMARY.
(Erase heading not required.)

Instructions regarding War Diaries and Intelligence Summaries are contained in F. S. Regs., Part II. and the Staff Manual respectively. Title pages will be prepared in manuscript.

Place	Date	Hour	Summary of Events and Information	Remarks and references to Appendices
			The attached, which should be considered as an Appendix to my War Diary for AUGUST, should be sent through the usual channels for approval up to same.	

3/9/19

M.C.C. Harrison Lieut. Colonel
Cmdg 17th R. Irish Regt.

With the kompliment of the Commanding Officer.

EXTRACT FROM:-

BATTALION ROUTINE ORDERS. NO. 757.

- by -

LIEUT. COL. W.H. CUNNINGHAM, D.S.O.

Commanding 2nd Battalion Wellington Regiment. 3/8/18.

- SPECIAL NOTICE -

The 2nd. Battalion of The Royal Irish Regiment, to which Regiment the 7th. Wellington West Coast Regiment is allied, are at present in Billets in ST. LEGER. Officers and O/Ranks of 7th. Wellington West Coast Company should visit their allied Regiment tomorrow, and make their acquaintance.

The friendship of the 18th. Royal Irish is greatly valued by the 7th. Regiment in New Zealand.

The 2nd. Battalion 18th. Royal Irish served in New Zealand during the Maori War, and had its Headquarters at Wanganui for a long period.

Special leave will be granted for above purpose.

2ND. BATTALION.
WELLINGTON REGIMENT.
NEW ZEALAND DIVISION.

SECRET.

188th. INF. BRIGADE WARNING ORDER No. 222.

1. Under instructions received from XVII Corps, the 63rd. Division will be prepared to relieve the 57th. Division in the left Sector on night 2nd./3rd. September.
   The 188th. Inf. Bde. will probably relieve the 170th. Inf. Bde. - H.Q. U.7.d.6.8.

2. Advanced reconnoitring parties of Battalions and 188th. L.T.M.Bty. will be conveyed by Motor Lorry which will be on the road outside the Brigade Camp at 9-00 a.m. to-morrow morning - 1st. September.

3. The 56th. Division (H.Q. S.11.a.5.7.) holds the Right Sector -

   167th. Inf. Bde. - H.Q. U.7.d.0.8.
   168th. Inf. Bde. - H.Q. U.7.d.8.4.
   169th. "   "   - H.Q. T.4.b.4.6.

4. The 1st. Canadian Division (Canadian Corps) is on the Left of 57th. Division, Headquarters WARLUS.

5. 170th. Inf. Bde. plus 2 Battalions 171st. Inf. Bde. holds the Left Sector.

6. The 57th. Division is covered by 5 Field Artillery Brigades and 2 Brigades R.G.A.

7. A good view of the forward area is obtainable from HENIN HILL, T.4.b. and d. and T.5.a. & c.

8. Please ACKNOWLEDGE BY BEARER.

Captain,
A/Brigade Major,
188th. Inf. Brigade.

31/8/18.

To all Units of Bde. Group.

18/63 2 R Irish Rg¹
WO 42
30.0.
(2 sheets)

Army Form C. 2118.

WAR DIARY
or
INTELLIGENCE SUMMARY.
(Erase heading not required.)

Instructions regarding War Diaries and Intelligence Summaries are contained in F.S. Regs., Part II. and the Staff Manual respectively. Title pages will be prepared in manuscript.

Place	Date	Hour	Summary of Events and Information	Remarks and references to Appendices
MONT ABLEUX-AU-	1/9/18	7/30 p.m.	Battalion left the camp and moved against the WOTAN SWITCH and spent the night in the assembly positions of (Hendecourt) HENDECOURT.	See App. 1
FONTAINE lès HENDECOURT	2/9/18	4/a.m.	Moved to jumping-off position — FONTAINE-LEZ-CROISILLES — Fontaine Wood of HENDECOURT.	
HENDECOURT		8/a.m.	Canadians having reported going successfully, 63 Divn: continued advance in rear of 57 Divn — who had orders to swing round and face south as soon as first Canadian objective had been reached. The Battalion eventually taking up its position along Railway line between CAGNICOURT and INCHY with Canadians on the left, Cavn: Bn: on the right.	
BOIS-DE-BOUCHE	3/9/18	4/30 a.m.	Companies were ordered to come back to our front in V.22.C. Here the Battalion concentrated and reformed. Battalion remained here in support to the 199 Bde. until the night of the 7. when they were relieved by the 9 Kings Liverpool 172 Bde of the 57 Divn:	

WAR DIARY
or
INTELLIGENCE SUMMARY.
(Erase heading not required.)

Army Form C. 2118.

Place	Date	Hour	Summary of Events and Information	Remarks and references to Appendices
BOIS-DE-BOUCHE	7/9/18	6.30 p.m.	On relief the Battalion marched to Warlus staying the night in Warlincourt line hult. The Warlus Factory.	
CROISILLES	8/9/18	6.30 p.m.	The Battalion marched to BOISLEUX-AU-MONT (By Rly) BOYELLES where they entrained for LAHERLIERE. On arrival the Battalion marched to Billets at GOUY-EN-ARTOIS arriving 12.30 a.m. 9/9/13.	
GOUY-EN-ARTOIS	9/9/18	11.30 a.m.	Battalion remained in billets (training) until the evening of the 17th, marching then to BLAIREVILLE, finishing up the march by a gentle attack on this village. Bn remained the night and, marched off at 10 a.m. to see ground East of Croisilles and ST LEGER finishing up by Bn Practice attack on ST LEGER Training here until	See App II and III.
	26/9/18		Bn remained in bivouacs	
	26/9/18 - 26/9/18			
CROISILLES	26/9/18	2.30 p.m.	Bn marched to assembly position immediately South of Bullecourt	

WAR DIARY or INTELLIGENCE SUMMARY

Army Form C. 2118.

Place	Date	Hour	Summary of Events and Information	Remarks and references to Appendices
LOEANT	27/9/18	12/45 a.m.	Bn. left the assembly positions and marched to jumping off point at Neuf St. C.N.E. D.2.c. at 6 P.M. Battalion marched to the assault, forming with the remainder of the Bn. the through the 9th Bn. The 8th the village of Graincourt) 3rd Rn C.P.R. in conjunction with the HAWKE Bn. The Bn. faced the night in sunken road E.30, A + C. to advance in rear of the 57 D.D. and	
GRAINCOURT	28/9/18	4 p.m.	The Bn. continued its advance through the 190 was billeted in Cambrai. And passing forward	
CANTAING	29/9/18	1 p.m.	Bn. continued its advance on position of last 57 B. N.W. BOÉ on the MARCOING LINE A 2.B. C + D. (came of last to establish a far as high ground A + B. confirmed attempt at CAMBRAI At 6.30 p.m. the Campi–Guarnieri–Cambrai M.G. fire compelled them Trenches across but line MASNIÈRES sent but our line to withdraw to our line Battalion in position as above.	
High Ground S of CAMBRAI	30/9/18	—		

WAR DIARY
or
INTELLIGENCE SUMMARY.
(Erase heading not required.)

Army Form C. 2118.

Place	Date	Hour	Summary of Events and Information	Remarks and references to Appendices
	24/9/18		Awards. PTE. J. MASON. 10869 L.C. D. O'REILLY. 10869 830 Tn. 18646 OC H. HOWE MILITARY 6260 PTE. P. ENGLISH. 9095. SGT. M. BERGIN. MEDAL 8536 PTE T.W. SLATER. Auth. No. A. 6/588 dated 21-9-18. Auth. Corps. letter. XVII 18589. QC A.G. CATLING. 18307. PTE. C. CROUCHER. 830. Cpl. G. LEWIS. 18524. L/S F. McCLARNON. 12190. L/C R. WELLS. 18574. L/C E. DELANEY 16208 L/C F. HUNT. 9113 PTE W. WARD. 8463 Cpl J. REID. 18336 Cpl J. CROWLEY. 8521 PTE R. BOGAN. 8482 PTE. J. HAYES 6137. PTE. C. O'GRADY. Bar to Military medal 18988. SGT. J. O'NEILL. M.M. Auth. IV Corps. letter No. SD/32 A. dated 20/9/18. Bar to Military medal. 11551. Q.S.M. S. NIXON. M.M. No SD/32 A. dated 21-9-18 Auth: IV Corps. letter	

Army Form C. 2118.

WAR DIARY
OR
INTELLIGENCE SUMMARY.
(Erase heading not required.)

Instructions regarding War Diaries and Intelligence Summaries are contained in F. S. Regs., Part II. and the Staff Manual respectively. Title pages will be prepared in manuscript.

Place	Date	Hour	Summary of Events and Information	Remarks and references to Appendices
	Week Ending 7/9/18		I. Casualties (a) Officers - 2/Lt A.C.C. Harrison R.E. W'ded. 2/Lt H.H. Arbuckle, C.F. Killed. Lt V.H. Lloyd, A.S.C. W'ded. Lt M.J. Hunt. W'ded. Capt B. Foulkes, W'ded. - all 2/9/18. (b) Other Ranks - Killed - 8; W'ded - 70 + Missing - 25.	
	Week Ending 30/9/18		(a) Officers - Lt W.H. Sanderson - W'ded 27/9/18. D'd 28/9/18 - Buried Cemetery - Bosleux-au-Mont. - 2/Lt R.W. Fitzgerald, R.D.F. W'ded - Lt H.L. North - Killed. 2/Lt R.E.W. Burke M.C. - W'ded - 2/Lt J.N. Robinson A.D.F. - all 27/9/18. Capt ?Em. T.F. Conrolly, R.D.M. - W'ded 28/9/18. 2/Lt D.D. Beckett C.R. - W'ded 30/9/18. (b) Other Ranks - Killed 33; W'ded 152. Missing 125. (a) Officers - 2/Lt A. Hope R.A.F. 2/Lt J.P. Butler, R.D.F. 2/Lt J. Shaw R.A.F. 2/Lt J. Bell R.D.F. 2/Lt J.W. Robinson R.A.F. 2/Lt R.C. Taylor, R.D.F. 2/Lt R.J. Fitzgerald R.D.F. 2/Lt W.S.W. Corrigan - all 8/9/18. - 2/Lt H.A. Sandys R.D.F. 14/9/18. Lt H.L. North, Lt L.R. McCarthy-Barry, Capt W.P. Hinton - all 20/9/18. Lt W. Tod. 2/Lt E.J. Short R.D.F - all 29/9/18. (b) Other Ranks - Week Ending 7/9/18 - 186 do 30/9/18 - 30	

7/10/18.

M.B. Ruttledge Lt Col.
Commanding 2/ Royal Irish Regiment

SECRET 2nd Bn Royal Irish Regt 17/9/18 Copy No 9

1. The Bn will continue the march tomorrow to the ST LEGER area.
2. Reveille 6 am Breakfasts 7 am
3. Order of march HQ
                    C Coy
                    D Coy
                    B Coy

4. The Bn will move off from present area at 8.45 am — H Q to pass the Starting point — Road junction X.4.b.5.9 at 9.15 am. Route to be notified later.
5. A distance of 200 yards will be maintained between Coys.
6. DRESS Fighting Order.
7. Packs, Officers' Valises etc will be dumped, by Coys, at the Transport Lines before 8 am.
8. Dinners will be served on the line of march. — Cookers, water carts, mess cart Lewis Gun Limbers will proceed immediately after Breakfast under 2/Lt MEANEY to road junction at T.14.b.0.7 — Dinners to be ready by 12.30 pm in field due WEST of above map Reference.
9. After the practice attack the Bn will be met by Guides at T.3.a.9.2.3

J.J. Reilly Capt & Adjt
2/Lt ? Act
Orders

3

Inter-Bn. Boundary - the E. and W. line thro'
V.3. central.

15. Instructions regarding the move of transport will be issued separately.

16. All Officers' Kits will be stacked on Guard Mounting Parade Ground by 11 a.m. T.O. will detail L.G. Limbers to report at Coy. HQrs. - Cookers will proceed with Coys. - cooking tea, and will return to Transport lines after tea.

17. Relief complete to be reported to Bn. HQrs. P.15.d.2.8. at once by runner.

18. Four Coys, T.O., Int. Off., Sig. Off. please ACKNOWLEDGE.

                        [signature]
                        Capt. & Adjt.
           2/ The Royal Irish Regt.

Issued at 8.30 p.m.

Copy No.				
1.	HQ 188 Bde.	9.	L.G.O.
2.	10/S. Foresters.	10.	Sig. Off.
3.	Sec-in-Comd.	11.	M.O.
4.	O/C A Coy	12.	Q.M.
5.	" B "	13.	T.O.
6.	" C "	14.	R.S.M.
7.	" D "	15.	Cook Sgt.
8.	Int. Off.	16.	War Diary.

No. 17 File.

SECRET. 2nd Royal Irish Regiment Orders No 32.   Copy No 15.

France sheet 51.6.} 1/40.000.   The Field 16-9-18
         51.C.}
         LENS. II

1. The 63rd (R.N.) Division (less Artillery) is relieving the 52nd Division in Support in the ST LEGER area.

2. The 188th Infantry Brigade Group marches to an area South of CROISILLES in T.30, staging on the night of the 17th inst at BLAIREVILLE and proceeding to CROISILLES from that place on the 18th inst.

3. On the 17th inst the Bn will proceed by march route to BLAIREVILLE.   Coys and Bn H.Q will parade outside billets at 9.15 am. and will pass the starting Point — X Roads Q.19.a.8.8.— at the following times:—

   Bn H.Q   9.30 am.
   'B' Coy   9.32 am.
   'C' Coy   9.34 am.
   'D' Coy   9.36 am.
   'A' Coy   9.38 am.

4. Route — MONCHIET — BEAUMETZ — GROSVILLE — BRETENCOURT — X Roads R.27.d.2.3. — BLAIREVILLE.

5. 200 Yards will be maintained between Infantry Companies and corresponding Units.   500 Yards will be maintained between Battalions.

6. First Line Transport of all units of the Group will proceed Brigaded under the Brigade Transport Officer.

7. BILLETS Billets will be left in a scrupulously clean condition and certificates to the effect that this has been done will be rendered to Bn H.Q by 6pm the 17th.

8. The usual billeting parties under LT. T. HUGHES will report to a representative of Bde. H.Q at 9 am the 17th inst at the Area Commandants Office, BLAIREVILLE

9. Officers Valises & men's Packs will be dumped by Coys at the Q.M. Stores by 7pm. on the 17th inst. Care must be taken to ensure that men's Packs are correctly marked with No, NAME and COY of Owner &

10. All moves will be carried out in Fighting Order, caps being neatly tied on to the haversack — any mess tins without covers will be put in the haversack.
11. ACKNOWLEDGE.

[signature]
Captain & Adjutant
2nd Bn The Royal Irish Regiment

Issued at 3 pm.
Copies to

1. Hd Qrs 188th Bde.
2. O/c "A" Coy
3. O/c "B" "
4. O/c "C" "
5. O/c "D" "
6. Asst Adjt
7. Int. Officer
8. M. O.
9. Q. M.
10. T. O.
11. Sigs Officer
12. R S M
13. Cook Sgt
14. War Diary
15. File
16. Spare
17. Spare

WAR DIARY
or
INTELLIGENCE SUMMARY.

Place	Date	Hour	Summary of Events and Information	Remarks and references to Appendices
	1-2	8.30	The Bn was relieved by a unit of the 52nd Division & marched into bivouacs just East of ANNEUX arriving at 11 PM	
	3-6		Time spent in reorganization & refitting. On the night of 6/7's 6th joined the Bn. During this period the Bn was subjected to continuous night bombing	

WAR DIARY
or
INTELLIGENCE SUMMARY.
(Erase heading not required.)

Army Form C. 2118.

Place	Date	Hour	Summary of Events and Information	Remarks and references to Appendices
	7/10/18	16.00	The Bn left the vicinity of ANNEUX and marched to assembly position west of RUMILLY arriving at 18.30. A hot meal was served at 23.39. The Bn then moved to its second assembly position North East of RUMILLY & were in position at 02.30 hours. Clear at 04.10. twenty minutes before zero	M/r
	8/10/18		The Bn moved to jumping off line. At 04.30 hours the Barrage opened & drew off on Bock flat line for 10 mins. When the Barrage lifted the Bn moved forward, keeping 150 yds behind barrage. The resistance was chiefly MG fire. The objective was reached at & occupied at 06.05 hours by all Coys. 3 Field Guns, 2 Trench Mortars numerous MG's & prisoners were taken by the Bn in its advance. The Wounded helped by the Stretcher Bearers reached their final objective in one & another hrs. at 08.00 hours. During the operations the Bn had one Tank attached to it. This Tank did ad-	

WAR DIARY
or
INTELLIGENCE SUMMARY.
(Erase heading not required.)

Army Form C. 2118.

Place	Date	Hour	Summary of Events and Information	Remarks and references to Appendices
	8/10/18	8.30	Initiated work silencing M.Gs. At 8.30 it was known our Bn. 8 was at enemy tanks ad. went on the direction of WAMBAIX completely attached vanguard. The advance of their infantry. All of them were British was explained by which hand had Cyan yo Ceders Tanks ex left ones which went knocked out. The others Sup of then south were knocked of by T.G. fire but returnes after leaving behind a Lt T.G. fire but returnest in the direction of Wambaix. At 16.15.30 hrs the enemy opened a heavy barrage and was at 16+ one tank accompanied by attacking infantry appeared Jun. tank was knocked out. Allied McCauly Batty fired an Auto Tank Gun. the infantry were getting within 100 yds of our line were easily driven back	AM1r
10/10/18	04.30	At 04.30 hours the Bn. was relieved by 9 East Surr Regt & marched back to held in front of ANNEUX at 12.15	
	12.15	At 12.15 the Bn. left & marched to ANNEUX MORCHIES arriving at 16.45hrs. The next two days were spent waiting	AM1r
12/10/18 13/10/18	8.00	The Bn. entrained at Vaux Vraucourt for St Pol arrived at 06.15 & marched to via fulleck at CROISETTE 6½ klo away	AM1r AM1r

Army Form C. 2118.

WAR DIARY
or
INTELLIGENCE SUMMARY.
(Erase heading not required.)

Instructions regarding War Diaries and Intelligence Summaries are contained in F.S. Regs., Part II. and the Staff Manual respectively. Title pages will be prepared in manuscript.

Place	Date	Hour	Summary of Events and Information	Remarks and references to Appendices
CROISETTE	13.10.18 to 21.10.18		The Bn spent this period in reorganisation and working. The Bn was occupied with a certain amount of light training, a bath in the morning. Soccer & other games took place in the afternoon. The weather was most uncertain. On the 20th October a Divl Gymkhana was held in St POL.	AM1 AM1 AM1 AM1
	22.10.18	9.30am	The Bn moved from billets in CROISETTE to billets in MAGNICOURT 8½ MILES away arriving at 1330 hours. Here the Bn commenced refresher training on the 23rd	AM1 AM1
	23.10.18		A BRIGADE Boxing Competition was held on the afternoon of the 23rd at MATIERES. The Bn won two weights	AM1
	24.10.18		A Divisional Race meeting was brought at LE CAUROY this date. The Bn won the ICO's Steeplechase of 2 miles	AM1
	26.10.18		The first round of the Brigade Soccer was played. The Bn beat 148th FdCoy RE AMBULANCE by 1-0	AM1 AM1
	27.10.18		The ground was played on Royal Marine Light Infantry beating our opponents the Bn won by 8-0	AM1
	28.10.18		A Brigade Cross country race of about 3½ miles was held. The Bn was not at full strength, many officers being on leave and "the Padre" 2nd the race was extremely heavy & every one was very done in at the end	AM1
	30.10.18		The first round of the Divisional Soccer was played. The Bn was not at full strength, Major O'Reilly being on leave and "The Padre" sick suffered a defeat by 1st Royal Fusiliers by 1-0	AM1

WAR DIARY
or
INTELLIGENCE SUMMARY.

(Erase heading not required.)

Army Form C. 2118.

Place	Date	Hour	Summary of Events and Information	Remarks and references to Appendices
	21.10.18		HONOURS AND AWARDS	
			Bar to MC	
			Captain R T Hamilton MC	
			Military Cross	
	9.10.18		Lieut W C D Gytten	
			2 Lieut J P Nolan	
			Lieut E A H Smith	MM
			Distinguished Conduct Medal	
			1683 Serg F Harrison	
			46.6 Corpl J Cogley MM	
	22.10.18		1984 Sgt A Sowers Bar to Military Medal	MM
			18584 Pte A Cathing 13004 Sgt F Watson DCM MM	
			16356 Sgt M Keating 16433 L/Cpl Military Medal	MM
			18585 A/Cpl Chapman 11030 A/Cpl F McCarthy 16193 A/Cpl S White	MM
			1982 L/Cpl E Merritt 16492 Pte F Clarke 16277 Pte N O'Connor	MM
			11427 A/Sgt D Moran 16558 Pte W Graves 16400 " N Murphy	MM
				16707 P Conway
			11615 Sgt E Skelly MM 2nd Bar to Military Medal	MM
	23.10		10412 Sgt W Robinson MM Bar to MM	MM
			6107 a/Sgt C Condon Military Medal	MM
			5830 Pte J Kelly 4207 Pte W Gormordy	
			18854 " J Kelly	

Army Form C. 2118.

WAR DIARY
or
INTELLIGENCE SUMMARY.
(Erase heading not required.)

Place	Date	Hour	Summary of Events and Information	Remarks and references to Appendices
			2 Lieut W McCredy Casualties Officers	
			" JP Butler (RDF) } Wounded in action 8.10.18	M'1
			Other Ranks	
			Killed in action 3	
			Wounded " 32	
			Missing " 9	
			Reinforcements	
			Captain AD Place MC Joined 11.10.18 + 75 Other Ranks 6.10.18	
			" JD Pickup (Leinster RC) " 13.10.18	M'1
			Lieut CH Morris (Leinsters) " 98.10.18	
			Departures	
			2 Lieut JH Corrigan to 5 The Royal Irish Regt 18.10.18	
			Lieut T Hughes (Connaught Rangers) App'd Instructor at Salonika - Struck off 25.10.18	

Mejr C Maddisonkirrof Col.
2 The Royal Irish Regiment

WAR DIARY
or
INTELLIGENCE SUMMARY.
(Erase heading not required.)

Army Form C. 2118.

2. R.I. Regt

Place	Date	Hour	Summary of Events and Information	Remarks and references to Appendices
	1/11/18		The Bn moved from Billets in MAGNICOURT to billets in EVIN-MALMAISON arriving at 1730 hrs. The Bn marched from MAGNICOURT to just outside PENIN where it entrained & proceeded to HENIN LIETARD, marching from there to #EVIN	
	2/11/18		Day spent in cleaning up billets which are quite good.	
	3/11/18		Final of Brigade Soccer between the Bn & ANSON, result scoreless draw.	
	4/11/18		Replay of final of Brigade Soccer, resulting in a win for the Regiment by 1-0. Scored by 2/Lieut BELL.	
	5/11/18		The Bn left EVIN-MALMAISON at 7AM & marched to the outskirts of AUBY where it entrained & was taken to HAULCHIN. This move took place in torrents of rain, everyone got soaked.	
	6/11/18		Moved again at 7AM to AULNOY in pours of rain	
	7/11/18		Left AULNOY at 9AM en route to SEBOURG, stopping at SAULTAIN for lunch which was badly handed to process & their very bad	
	8/11/18		Marched from SEBOURQUIAUX through ANGRES then on to AUBREGNIES.	
	9/11/18		Bn moved to Nr AUBREGNIES, stopping at Bt AGGIES for lunch, then going on to SARS-LA-BRUYERE Hd.Qrs. when billetted in the Chies' Lodge where Gen Sir Horace SMITH DORRIEN was in 1914. Hd.Qrs had a dug-out of tea & dinner prepared with a badge button visiual in a bag of the Regiment which is to be placed in the Church after the war.	App I
	10.11.18		The Bn Moved from SARS-LA-BRUYERE leap-frogging the 190 "Brigade on side NOUVELLES then continuing the pursuit of retreating enemy. No hostiles M.G fire was encountered intact an advance of about 8 kilos was made.	
	11.11.18		An armistice has been signed & hostilities ceased at 11am today. The Bn had advanced as far as SPIENNES a/ad & shots since tuesday & following in enemy the Bn were quartered in Spiennes	App II

(A10266) Wt. W5300/P173. 750,000 2/18 Sch. 53 Forms/C2115/16. D.D.& L., London, E.C.

WAR DIARY or INTELLIGENCE SUMMARY

Army Form C. 2118.

Place	Date	Hour	Summary of Events and Information	Remarks and references to Appendices
SPIENNES	12.11.18		No news. The battalion for ages, everyone resting, in very good spirits. Rating, cleaning up. Regimental Dinners in Mons in celebration of peace.	A1
	13.11.18		Commanding Officer awarded DSO. Major General Hull came to lunch & afterwards took up some of the officers round the Mons battlefield. A large number of presents to the men of the Regiment also Captain for big number were found. The Bn ended the week in practically the same spot as they started.	A1
	14.11.18			A1
	15.11.18		Official entry into Mons by the Gen. the Army Commanding 1st Army Corps (Hon...) Colthurst DSO MC, Capt AR Place MC, Capt Nev gadbury MC, Capt Hayto. Recent attended. JHA N. VLD 250 men were selected to be led by the Bn.	A1
	16.11.18		Today buzzoners of war commenced to arrive from Germany. Two were taken into the Bn. arrived at GIVRY came over to be the Bn. had been taken on the 21st March 1918. The others were of the Regt.	A1
	17.11.18		More preparations on wing in. So for have 4 of the Regt.	A1
	18.11.18		Two more Royal Irish Regt inter prisoners arrived.	A1
	19-21		Nothing of importance - inter company football in the afternoon. Bn. went to a royal march. Visited the Mons Battlefield. Men were very interested but there were only a very few remaining of those actually who were there in 1914.	A1
	22-26		Nothing of importance.	A1
	27		Bn. left SPIENNES at 10.00 hours. The villagers all turned out to see us go. As we were very popular in this village. Marches App IV NOUVELLES - ASQUILLIES - NOIRCHAIN and GENLY to byelets in HARGNIES Arrived about 14.00. Billets are fairly good but populace are not as nice as the "SPIENNOISE"	A1

WAR DIARY
or
INTELLIGENCE SUMMARY

Army Form C. 2118.

Place	Date	Hour	Summary of Events and Information	Remarks and references to Appendices
BLAREGNIES	28		Our Brigadier, Br. Genl. T.D. COLERIDGE CMG DSO, recalled to India. All ranks were sorry at losing this most popular Brigadier. The command of the 188th Infy Bde was taken over by Bt-Genl H. NELSON DSO (Border Regt)	App V
	29		Uneventful	
	30		Seems barks to H.C. The Military Cross	V
			HONOURS AND AWARDS	
			— Capt G.O.F. ALLEY MC RAMC	
			— Lieut W. TOD	
			" L.R. McCARTHY-BARRY	
			The Distinguished Conduct Medal — 7061 A/Sgt. McLEOD. G	
			The Military Medal — 9886 A/CSM UPSON. A.E.	
			The Distinguished Service Order — Lt. Col. M.C. HARRISON. MC	
			OFFICERS — JOININGS	V
			2/Lieut W.H. GOOD MC (The Connaught Rangers) 21-11-18	
			" J.H. GREHAN (RDF) 24-11-18	
			" W. CAHILL	
			" A.V. HALLEWELL Somerset Light Infy "	
			2/Lieut R.D. MARTIN "	
			" W.G.M. PARFITT "	
			" H. ROWE "	
			" A.E. WARREN "	
			OFFICERS — DEPARTURES	
			Capt. A.V. BRIDGE wounded in action 10-11-18	
			Lieut J.P. MARREN "	
			2/Lieut N.S.W. CORRIGAN "	
			" M.J. MEANEY "	
			" J. BELL (RDF) "	

M.C. Harrison
LIEUT. COLONEL,
COMMANDING 2nd Bn. THE ROYAL IRISH REGT.

Appendix 1

2nd Royal Irish Regiment
Summary of Events from 9/11/18 to 11/11/18

9th Nov.   188 I.y B'de is in support to 190
           who are advancing with little opposition
           on NOUVELLES — HARVENG ROAD
0500   Batt'n arrives in billets at Bruery
           in SARS LA BRUYERE.

10th Nov.
0600   Operation order issued
0700   Batt'n 188 B'de group proceeds via
           BOUGNIES to ASQUILLIES
0800   (illegible) C.O. at Conference in 190 B'de H.Q.
           Batt'n arrives at ASQUILLIES &
           forms up on eastern side of
           line near MALADRIE
1100   hour fixed for 188 B'de to pass
           through 190. Royal Irish on left, Hawke
           Batt'n on right & Royal Marines in
           support. As O.C. Anson Batt'n
           reported unable to push immediately the

10th. line before 12:15 hours it was decided by O.C's leading battalions to cross NOUVELLES — HARVENG road at 12:30 hours

10:30 Hostile heavy artillery very active on ASQUILLIES till 12:30

12:30 Battn passed through 170 Bde
B Coy on left   D Coy on right
A Coy in Support   C Coy in reserve

01:15 B. Coy encountered serious opposition from M.G's on railway embankment on their front & also from left flank.

01:45 B & D Coys had reached a line from 200-300 yards from railway. Three different attempts were made to advance from this position but owing to artillery & heavy machine gun fire it was impossible to make any progress in battn sector.

02.00   It was observed at 02.00 hours that Anson battn had succeeded in forcing a passage over river & railway on right of our D Coy & appeared to be advancing successfully on first objective. C Coy (Reserve Coy) Royal Irish was at once launched with orders to force their way through this gap & push on to Royal Irish first objective with all speed. B & D Coys being ordered to cooperate with this flanking move

02.45   This operation was partially successful C Coy having reached the high ground east of railway & river in battn sector the enemy was obliged to abandon the line of the railway in front of B & D Coys.

05.30   As both flanks had become exposed and enemy continued to sweep all open ground with machine gun fire further advance by day without adequate artillery support appeared to be out of the question.

Orders were accordingly issued for the advance to be continued at 0600 hours. B & D Coys to consolidate in MALPLAQUET. C Coy to consolidate in CHEMICAL WORKS on MALPLAQUET — HARMIGNIES ROAD A Coy to consolidate on Northern outskirts of SPIENNES

10.00   All objectives were reached

12.00   Patrols entered SAINT-SYMPHORIEN & found it deserted by enemy.

Our casualties
- 6 officers wounded
- 53 O.R wounded
- 4 O.R killed
- 6 O.R missing

Prisoners captured 1 wounded O.R.
Several German dead were found in battalion sector including one officer.
2 M.G.s captured on railway embankment.

M.C.C. Harrison Lt Col
Cmdg 2nd R.I. Rgt

12/11/18

63rd Div. Arty.	63rd Div. Train.	Corps Mntd. Troops.
63rd Div. Engs.	A. A. & Q. M. G.	16th Lancers.
63rd Div. Sigs.	D.A.D.M.S.	D.A.D.O.S.
188th Inf. Bde.	D.A.P.M.	D.A.D.V.S.
189th Inf. Bde.	Camp Commandant.	Div. Recptn. Camp.
190th Inf. Bde.	63rd Div. Rear.	M.T.Coy.
63rd M.G.Battn.	63rd Mob. Vet. Sec.	D.G.O.
14/Worcs. Regt.	S.A.A.Section.	Div. Employ. Co.
		O/C. N.Z. Cyclists.

G.419.   11th.   AAA

Hostilities will cease at 11.00 hours Nov. 11th AAA All troops will stand fast on line reached at that hour which will be reported to D.H.Q. AAA All defensive precautions will be maintained and an outpost line established AAA There will be no parleying with the enemy who if he attempts to come over will be sent back by an officer AAA Addsd. all concerned.

— *C H Blackock* —

08.30 hours.   Major General,
                                    Commanding, 63rd (RN) Division.

SPECIAL ORDER OF THE DAY.
BY
Lieut. Colonel M.C.C. HARRISON. D.S.O, M.C.,
Commanding 2nd Bn. THE ROYAL IRISH REGIMENT......

I wish to thank all ranks for the magnificent way in which they fought on the 10th. inst.

The enemy was holding an exceptionally strong position, and the battalion, by reaching all objectives before the units on either flank, has maintained to the last the high fighting reputation of the oldest Irish Regiment –
"The Gallant 18th."

The Field
13th. Nov. 1918.

M. C. C. Harrison
Lieut. Colonel.

War Diary

To all ranks of the 188th. Infantry Brigade.

      I wish to place on record my high appreciation of the splendid gallantry shown by all ranks during the action of the 10th. instant.

      After long marches in bad weather, a most formidable position, stubbornly defended, was carried. This, in itself, was no mean achievement and was all the more meritorious as it was performed when rumours of the cessation of hostilities were rife and it was realized that the action might prove the last battle of the war.

      May the forthcoming peace, which you have so bravely helped to win, be happy and prosperous for you all.

J.X. Coleridge
Brigadier General,
Commanding - 188th. Infantry Brigade.

12th. Nov., 1918.

APP C

2nd Bn The Royal Irish Regiment Order No. 33. Copy No ___

Map Valenciennes 1/40000 ___ In the Field 26.11.18

1. The Bn will move to billets in BLAREGNIES tomorrow the 27th inst.
2. Starting point: Railway Crossing at O.34.c.7.9.
3. Coys will pass the starting point in the following order at the following times:—
    DRUMS.   10-00 hours.
    Bn HQ.   10-00 "
    "D" Coy.   10-02 "
    "C" "   10-04 "
    "A" "   10-06 "
    "B" "   10-08 "
    TRANSPORT. 10-10 "
    Route as below.
4. All cookers and their ___ will move off at 08-30 hours under Lt. R. ADAMSON. This party will proceed direct to BLAREGNIES.
5. Blankets (rolled in bundles of ___ and carefully labelled) and packs will be dumped outside the GUARD ROOM at 07-30 hours. If wet they will be dumped in Canteen. Officers Valises will be dumped outside the GUARD ROOM at 08-30 hours.
6. A billeting party, consisting of the 5 C.Q.M.S. and 1 N.C.O for the Transport will report to CAPT. J.F. O'REILLY outside the H.Q. Mess at 08-45 hours. This party will proceed by march route.
7. Dress:— Fighting Order with Caps.
8. Billets and their surroundings must be left scrupulously clean. Certificates, signed by O.C. Coys and Lieut D. BISSETT ___ (for H.Q. Coy) will be handed to the ADJUTANT by 09-30 hours.
9. Lieut. J.H.A. NEVILL will remain behind to deal with any claims which may be brought forward by the inhabitants.
10. Routine. Reveille 06-30 hours. ___ at 7-30 hours
    Sick Parade 08-30 hours.
11. Route ___

    ___ Capt & Adjt
    2nd Royal Irish Regiment.

Copies to
1 Second in Command.
2   " A Coy
3   " B "
4   " C "
5   " D "
6 Int Officer
7 M.O.
8 Q.M.
...
11 Lt NEVILL
12 R.S.M.
13 ___ Sgt
14 War Diary
15 File

App V

To all Ranks of 188th Infantry Brigade.

On the occasion of my recall to India I wish to say "Good bye" to you all and to thank you for your gallant and stedfast conduct during the past memorable year we have served together.

I am convinced that no Commander has ever been better served, and I am proud to have commanded such a Brigade, which, undismayed by adverse fortune earlier in the year, was ever ready to attack and defeat the enemy, when good fortune came our way this autumn.

May your future prove as prosperous as your past has proved distinguished.

J. D. Coleridge
Brigadier-General,
Commanding,
188th Infantry Brigade.

SG/A/1534.
27th November 1918.

WAR DIARY or INTELLIGENCE SUMMARY

Army Form C. 2118.

(Erase heading not required.)

2 Bn R. Irish Regt. 9/18

Place	Date	Hour	Summary of Events and Information	Remarks and references to Appendices
BLAREGNIES	1-12-18		H.M. The King & H.R.H. The Prince of Wales who were inspecting the Bn were introduced to the Coy O.C.s & Sen. NCOs on the 6th June A.G. O'Brien 2 Lieut D Boal D.C.M. M.M., CSM Upton MM, Sgt Garvey M.M., Sgt Cosby DCM M.M. proceeded to Clonmel MM	
	7-12-18		The Divisional Commander inspected the 188th Brigade on the Plaine G.O.C.	
	8-12-18		On the 8th a party of Officers & NCOs went to see the battlefield of Mons & also the Bn was moved by buses whilst interesting sights were seen on the 13th Bn moved to FRAMERIES	
FRAMERIES	14.12.18		Sporting games & educational parades were carried on	
"	15.12.18			
"	21.12.18			
"	22.12.18		The Colours arrived out. Christmas Day – "the best yet". The dinner was a great success	
"	25.12.18			
"	26-31		26 Volunteers were demobilized during the latter part of the month. All men going on leave were in civilian clothes. There is nothing to record during the month. Other than in States above the keep work has invariably been Education and Ceremonial	

M.C.H. Hemphill Col.
Cmdr of the Royal Irish Regt

Army Form C. 2118.

WAR DIARY
or
INTELLIGENCE SUMMARY
(Erase heading not required.)

Instructions regarding War Diaries and Intelligence Summaries are contained in F. S. Regs., Part II. and the Staff Manual respectively. Title pages will be prepared in manuscript.

Hour, Date, Place	Summary of Events and Information	Remarks and references to Appendices
Francisco 1-7.11.19	The Bn. Tug of War team beat the Drake Bn in the final (Billetown) Capt. Weight got trooped up in the morning sports, in the afternoon during the walk the tug-o-war team was held in Biskailea. Ho 6"	
8-14.11.19	The Bn. Band arrived at home bre on the 13th Trophy Inspections carried out 3 days a week & concert parties. Fr is 9 the Off mess gave a dance on the 14th	
15-21.11.19	Having no concerts hand, officers & men staged a corps date on the 18th which was much enjoyed, some officers from the 8th came for the day	
22-29.11.19	The Bn. tug of war team beat the Corps competition team on Tuesday 22 Nov in the final by a bundle. A cup & dance held on the 25. Heavy fall of snow prevents match between 5th Bn & Drake taking place. Weather very cold	

M. C. C. Harrison Lieut-Col
Omdg 2nd R. I. Rgt.

Army Form C. 2118.

WAR DIARY
or
INTELLIGENCE SUMMARY.

(Erase heading not required.)

Instructions regarding War Diaries and Intelligence Summaries are contained in F. S. Regs., Part II. and the Staff Manual respectively. Title pages will be prepared in manuscript.

Place	Date	Hour	Summary of Events and Information	Remarks and references to Appendices

Honours & Awards

Captain A V Budge MC Bar to MC
" " Major J Evans (auth'y ARO 434 of 27.12.18)
" " J F O'Reilly M'day Coin
Lieutenant R Adamson M'day Coin

5640 Pte O'Dea awarded DCM
18307 Pte Crawley Bar to MM's
16358 " Gurvee "
8518 R.Q.M.S Hopkins " and London Gaz 18.1.19
9637 Pte Dickinson "

Promotion
8508 a/CSM Mellows H.D. Coy to be CSM with effect from 27.9.18
12240 a/CSM Keating M.M A Coy " " " " 25.10.18
6487 Sgt Cutford E Coy " a/CQMS " " " 5.1.19
16387 L/C Charod T Coy " " " " "

34 O.
2 sheets

M.C.C. Harrison Lieut Col
Comdg 2nd R.I.Rgt.

WAR DIARY or INTELLIGENCE SUMMARY

Army Form C. 2118.

Place	Date	Hour	Summary of Events and Information	Remarks and references to Appendices
Francières	Feb		On the 5th the Bn marched to Mons to attend a Requiem Mass in the Cathedral for Officers & Men of the Regt fallen in the War. The Revd Fr Kane MCCF officiated. Snow has been on the ground since the end of Jany. Ceremonial parades have been unable to be [carried?] out. 870 Other Ranks under Capt H P Hutton proceeded to the 9th Regt of 10th [?] on 13.2.19 for Army of Occupation. They proceeded to Boulogne. 2 B. [?] won the One Cross Country Race held on 22nd. The Divisional Rugby Cup. [?] was also won on the 27th 2 B. [?] was held at the following. M. [?] by the 93 Bde and on 13th 2 KN IOU Demolition [?] was going on at a [?] 13th. Leaving extremely weak.	
			Arrivals	
			NIL Departures	6.2.19
				7.2.19
			Capt J R Pickup } To concert Camp for demob	
			3 " E S Hunter " " "	
			Capt H. J. Hunton }	
			Lieut J F O'Reilly	
			" J F McCauley · Barry } To 1st The Royal Ir. Regiment
			" J F Leahy on 13.2.19 for Army of Occupation
			" E C Salway · Foley
			" O/E Swanwick
			" Q/E Adamson
			2 " R Q Boisragon
			" J H Pigott
			12 " Martin
			870 Other Ranks	

M O C [Ramsey?]
LIEUT. COLONEL,
COMMANDING 2nd Bn. THE ROYAL IRISH REGT.

WAR DIARY
or
INTELLIGENCE SUMMARY.
(Erase heading not required.)

Army Form C. 2118.

2 R Irish R

Place	Date	Hour	Summary of Events and Information	Remarks and references to Appendices
FRAMERIES	1-30 March		A was received that "Demobilization practically complete & the Bn very heavily down to cadre strength although 9's men further past battn are away having 2 weeks leave. 13 months leave to Ireland or 2 weeks leave to those taking up discharge in England. We came out of 2 Welsh Regiment on 30" proceeded to give men all our equipment. We are now awaiting orders to proceed to England. During the two with 3rd RMLI heal we was a soccer by 3-0 goals, but held a very wide lead in 2nd. 9's a players having been demobilised & beat an beat us at hockey twice the 3-2 and 4-2 goals. Departure Officers 2 Lieut A Coventry To UK for 2 months leave faulty AG 86538 (0) 4/21.1.19 Capt G of Airey MC (RAMC) To 148 Field Ambulance Capt E A W Smith MC (Cargh Rangers) To UK (2 month leave 15.3.19 2/Lt H A Saunders (RAF) Released in UK for demob " JH A Hunt (Spec list) To Concentration Camp for demob (LS) 20.3.19 2/Lt PMC Quate Lieut WH Good MC (CR) } To S R Ir Regiment 19.3.19 2/Lt J A Graham (RAF) Lieut W C D Guffin MC } To Concentration Camp for demob 24.3.19 2/Lt JD Kelly 2/Lt W Croft 2/Lt W Cahill (RAF) To S R Ir Regiment 26.3.19 Lieut A Tod MC } To concentration Camp for demob 27.3.19 (LS) Lieut Q I Rowlette (CR) " 30.3.19 (1) 10 Ranks 100 O Ranks left the Bn during the month either for demobilization or proceeding on re-enlistment leave	36 F. 1 sheet

M. C.C. Harris
LIEUT. COLONEL
COMMANDING 2nd Bn. THE ROYAL IRISH REGT.

WAR DIARY
or
INTELLIGENCE SUMMARY.
(Erase heading not required.)

Army Form C. 2118.

Place	Date	Hour	Summary of Events and Information	Remarks and references to Appendices
France	1-4-19 to 30-4-19		A very uneventful month. Lieut Col Harman left the Bn on 5-4-19. Proceeded to S.B. to take over temporary command. Major O'Reilly took over command of the Cadre of the Bn. We are now awaiting orders to proceed home.	Closed
	2-5-19		No orders to come in. We proceed on the 4th to Rugeley Camp Stafford.	

M. O'Reilly Major
Comdg. 2 The Royal Irish Regiment

www.ingramcontent.com/pod-product-compliance
Lightning Source LLC
Chambersburg PA
CBHW082013220426
43670CB00014B/2613